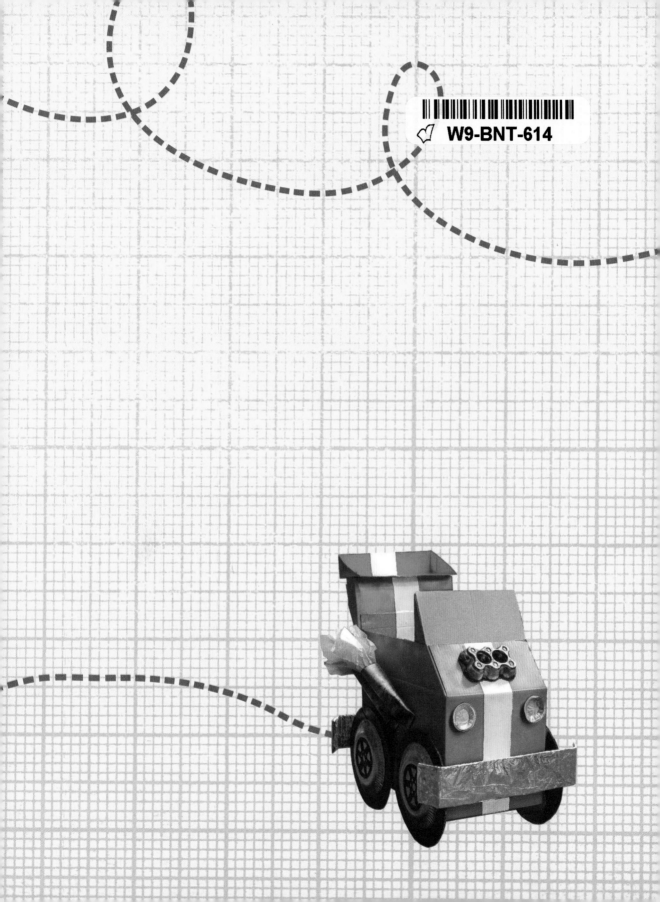

PROJECT DAD

MAKE EVERY DAY AN ADVENTURE WITH DAD!

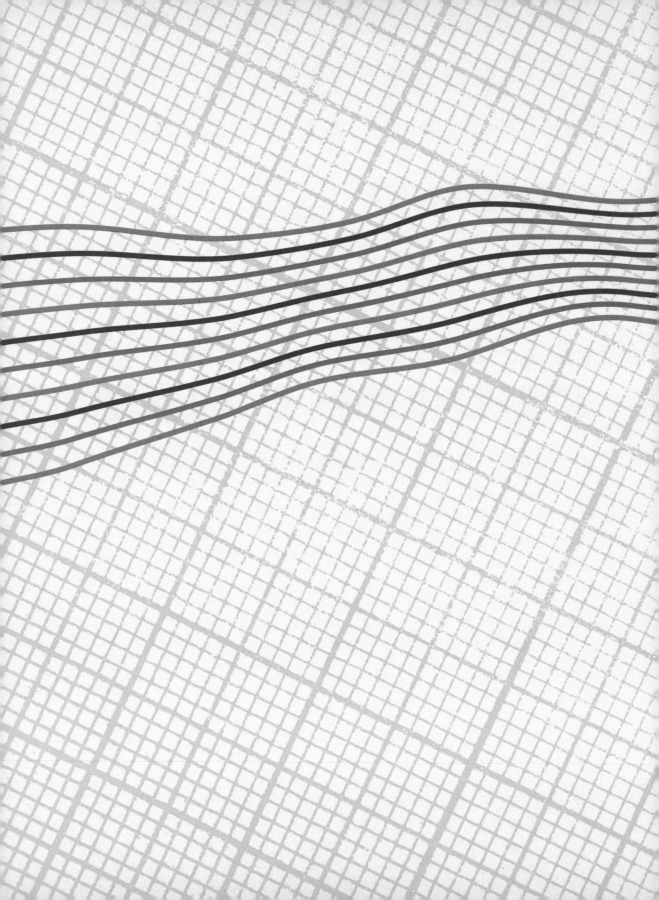

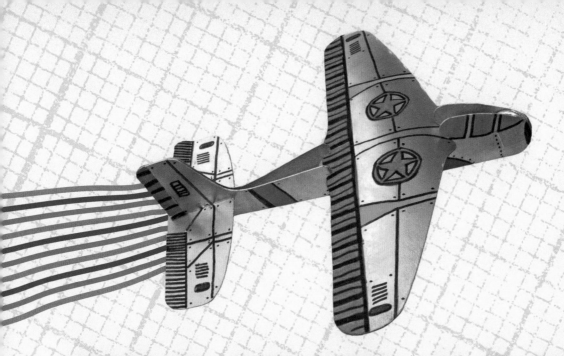

PROJECT DAD

MAKE EVERY DAY AN ADVENTURE WITH DAD!

PaRragon

Bath • New York • Singapore • Hong Kong • Cologne • Delhi
Melbourne • Amsterdam • Johannesburg • Shenzhen

This edition published by Parragon Books Ltd in 2015

Parragon Inc.
440 Park Avenue South, 13th Floor
New York, NY 10016
www.parragon.com

Written by Lee Coan and Diane Ashmore
Illustrated by Dynamo
Designed by Lexi L'Esteve and Rhys Prosser
Project photos by Henry Sparrow
Project managed and edited by Cheryl Warner

Text on how to build a shelter and how to build a campfire has been provided by Paul Weller of
Keswick Canoe and Bushcraft
Monster Truck on page 106 is modeled by Harry Voss

ISBN 978-1-4723-8105-7
Printed in China

Contents

Contents

Fun at Home

INTRODUCTION

Imagine being able to drive your own Monster Truck, being a knight or princess in your own castle, or being able to check some bugs into your own bug hotel. This book brings your child's imagination to life with 20 projects that any daring Dad can make with or for a child. From being a great explorer, camping out in the wilds of your own backyard, to making a puppy pom-pom, there's a variety of activities to choose from that will please any child.

The only predictable thing about the weather is that it is unpredictable, so activities for rainy days are as valuable as those for discovering the great outdoors. This book contains two sections: one to cover outdoor activities and the other to usefully cover activities for around the home. Not that home-base activities are any less adventurous—making a target and catapult is just as fun and exciting as going on a scavenger hunt. Once you've made the target and catapult, there are endless games to play as you get better at hitting the target.

The crafts and activities in this book are designed for Dad to make and involve a child where he thinks appropriate. For example, Dad can do all of the cutting and gluing for the castle project and involve his little helper in decorating and painting the castle. For the shadow puppet theater, Dad could cut out the shapes and help glue them together, but the design of the puppets, the gripping story line, and the star performance is entirely the child's. Playing in the castle or creating a shadow puppet play will make the time fly by. The idea is to work as a team, creating imaginative projects that can make life-size toys for hours of fun afterward.

Discovering the great outdoors is made into a big adventure with advice on creating a campfire, camping out in the wilds of your own backyard, or becoming the next intrepid explorer with your own special equipment. Exciting worlds can unfurl with the aid of seemingly mundane objects. With an explorer kit, you and your child can go on wild adventures with just an old suitcase, a magnifying glass, an old map, and a dash of imagination. Camping out can incorporate a whole host of activities, including outdoor games, talking on metal-can telephones, or stargazing. You could even create the outdoor shelter instead of using a tent for a whole day of outdoor activity.

Discovering the outdoors doesn't need to be confined to your own backyard. The beach can become a magical place if you spend the day beachcombing, searching for critters in tide pools, or building a sandy version of a snowman—made from sand (obviously), with seaweed for hair and a pebble for the nose. You could even take the children on a scavenger hunt, giving them a list of items to find, or they could make a nature scrapbook to record their discoveries.

Not all activities need a long list of tools to make them. The Imaginative Questions activity merely involves writing your questions on paper, wrapping them into swirls, and inserting them in a jar to be unfurled at any time to spark up a conversation. To give your child a boost of confidence, get them to create an "I Am Great" self-portrait. They can even make it as part of a time capsule to be uncovered years later. Whatever you or your child's interests may be, there is something in this book for everyone.

START CRAFTING!

Craft activities don't have to be expensive or time-consuming. You can collect everyday household items, such as cardboard boxes, beverage cartons, cereal boxes, and even cardboard tubes from rolls of paper towels to use in your projects. You don't need to spend a lot, and it's also a great lesson on how to reuse items that are destined for the garbage dump—transforming them with just a little imagination into great play activities.

 The "Dad Only" symbol used in the projects helps give guidance on what needs to be done by an adult. The idea is that you make the projects with your child, deciding when it is safe to involve them. The "Dad Only" symbol usually highlights activities that include cutting, using a hot glue gun, and anything else that may involve sharp edges or hot materials. Children can help to draw out shapes or stick things together with double-sided tape or craft glue instead. They will also have loads of fun using their creativity to decorate the projects.

Each project includes a list of items that you'll need. Most of them are items that you'll have around the home, but the list also includes the tools that you will need to make the project.

Some of the craft projects involve the use of a glue gun, which, although fun to use, should be used only by an adult, because the glue gets hot. Glue guns, available from craft stores, are great for a quick-drying, secure adhesive that can be used for many types of materials. Solid glue sticks are inserted into the tool, which heats the glue and transforms it from solid to liquid. In its hot liquid state, handle the glue with care. The glue cools quickly and as it dries, it becomes solid again, providing a secure grip.

White craft glue takes much longer to dry, and surfaces will sometimes need holding in place while it dries. Children can safely use white glue and there are brands that are designed to wash out more easily from clothes. Another option is to use double-sided tape, which is great for attaching paper or cardboard surfaces that are not too heavy. Just secure to one of the surfaces, remove the film of paper on top, and then attach the other surface.

In many of the projects, you'll also need to use a craft knife, utility knife, or scissors, which again should be used only by an adult. When cutting with a craft or utility knife, it is a good idea to protect your work surface either with a cutting mat or, if you don't have one of those, a piece of thick corrugated cardboard (anything thick enough to protect the surface from cutting will do). Alternatively, you could use a workbench that you don't mind getting scratched on the surface or splashed with paint.

When using white glue or paint, getting your child to wear old clothes or some kind of apron or overall is a great idea, so there will be no need to worry about ruining any clothes. Protecting surfaces with old newspapers or thick cardboard, if needed, means that you and your child can enjoy making the projects without worrying about damage to furniture.

The idea is to have fun making the craft projects safely, and to have hours of fun with the finished results. Once you've mastered the basic designs, you can personalize these projects, using pens, crayons, or paints. You could even try collaging some of the projects, such as the Monster Truck, by cutting pictures out of magazines and attaching them with white glue. The possibilities are endless!

ACTIVITIES FOR THE GREAT OUTDOORS

You can't beat getting out of the house to go on adventures, finding worlds waiting to be discovered. In this book, there are various activities to spark your child's imagination and while away the hours outside. You don't even have to go that far—adventures lie right on the doorstep, in your own backyard, or you could just visit the nearest park.

There are many types of habitat that you can use or make to attract wildlife to your yard, from birdhouses, birdbaths, and toad houses to the simple and easy-to-make bug hotel described on page 18. A homemade bug hotel is guaranteed to check in some interesting creepy-crawly critters. All you need is a flowerpot and a few bug-friendly materials.

Camping out doesn't have to be a long drive away to a spot in the middle of nowhere. You can pitch a tent or make a shelter in your own backyard (see page 38). This is a great opportunity for stargazing and a chance to identify the important constellations. You don't need a fancy telescope to do this—there's a lot to see just with the naked eye. It could ignite a fascination for space in your child that lasts for years to come.

The best part about camping is the games and activities surrounding it. If you can't decide which games to play first, create an "Activity Jar." Everyone gets to write down their favorite games on pieces of paper, fold them up, and place them in a jar. Then take turns picking from the jar to see what you get to play.

Creating an explorer kit (see page 34) is a great way of initiating various games or activities. With your explorer kit ready, you could try playing "I Spy," describing animals or plants you come across as you roam and getting others to guess the name. Or if there are enough people to take part, you could create two teams, each team scoring points for finding items on a list. The winners are the ones who spot everything first.

Making a nature scrapbook (see page 46) can spark an interest in art as well as nature. With just a few crayons and a piece of paper, you could take rubbings of different types of bark, for example, securing them in the scrapbook as you go along. With just a pencil, or a few colored pencils, you could draw whatever catches the eye as you take a walk. Write up a brief description, the time, and the place to record what you've found.

Making a glider (see page 30) or a kite (see page 50) is just the beginning of an adventure. After decorating them with your favorite colors, it's time to visit the park. You could make two or more kites or gliders and have races with them. Remember to fly your glider or kite on a day with a gentle breeze for the best results, allowing it to fly farther and stay in one piece.

Vacations can be a great time to play outdoor games. A visit to the beach provides plenty of scope for activities involving all the family. As well as making the sand man, mentioned on page 58, you could collect pebbles and make them into pictures in the sand. Or build a car in the sand, large enough to sit in. Try making a dam or even a channel to be filled up by water as it crashes on the beach.

ACTIVITIES FOR AROUND THE HOME

A day around the home doesn't have to mean a dull day. This section of the book will arm you with a range of activities and craft projects to keep your child occupied for hours. You don't need to have lots of fancy toys or equipment—just a simple afternoon spent baking in the kitchen can provide hours of entertainment for you and your child.

The crafts and activities in this book are mainly designed for Dad to make, using the "Dad Only" symbol as a guide and involving a child where you think appropriate. Dad will do most of the cutting and gluing with the glue gun, but children will love decorating the projects and can personalize them to their heart's content. Use water-base craft paints, which are easy to wash away and nontoxic, thick felt-tip pens or crayons.

The Crusher-Bot Puppet (see page 80) offers a great opportunity for imaginative decoration. Paint his teeth white and add eyelashes to his table tennis-ball eyes. You could use silver water-base paint or glue and cover him with aluminum foil to give him a robotic metallic finish.

The Monster Truck (see page 106) would look fantastic painted racing red or covered with squares of tissue paper or pictures cut from a magazine. You could also paint a layer of white glue on top to give it a sheen.

Let your child be the king or queen of the castle with the project on page 62. They can decorate it with colored pens or pencils or glue pictures of knights or princesses onto the sides—no doubt they will probably want to also dress up as a little princess or prince.

Making a shadow puppet theater is more than just a craft project. Once you've made the theater (see page 100) and the screen to capture the shadow, it's time to create the puppets and a story to tell. You don't just have to stick to a simple black silhouette; you could use a doll, a twig, your hand and fingers, or anything that has an interesting shape. Why not use the sock caterpillar (see page 112) as a shadow puppet? Use a table lamp as a light source or a flashlight that can be moved to change the shape of the shadow.

Let your imagination run wild when it comes to the story or try a simple fairy tale. One person can move the puppets, another could read out the story, and, of course, you need to invite other members of the family or friends to an exclusive performance as the audience.

Once you've made the catapult and target (see page 72), screw up some balls of old newspaper and get practicing. When you've got the hang of it, have a game of who can hit the target the most number of times, increasing the challenge by moving the target farther and farther away.

Activities to do at home can be as simple as drawing with crayons. You could pencil in some shapes for them to color or help them to draw their own designs. If they are not enthusiastic about drawing, finger painting is also a great option. Just make sure to cover all surfaces and have them wear old clothes. A great game is to draw a character's head on a piece of paper and fold it over so that the next person can see only the bottom of the head. Then that person draws the arms and the next draws a body and legs. The results can be hilarious!

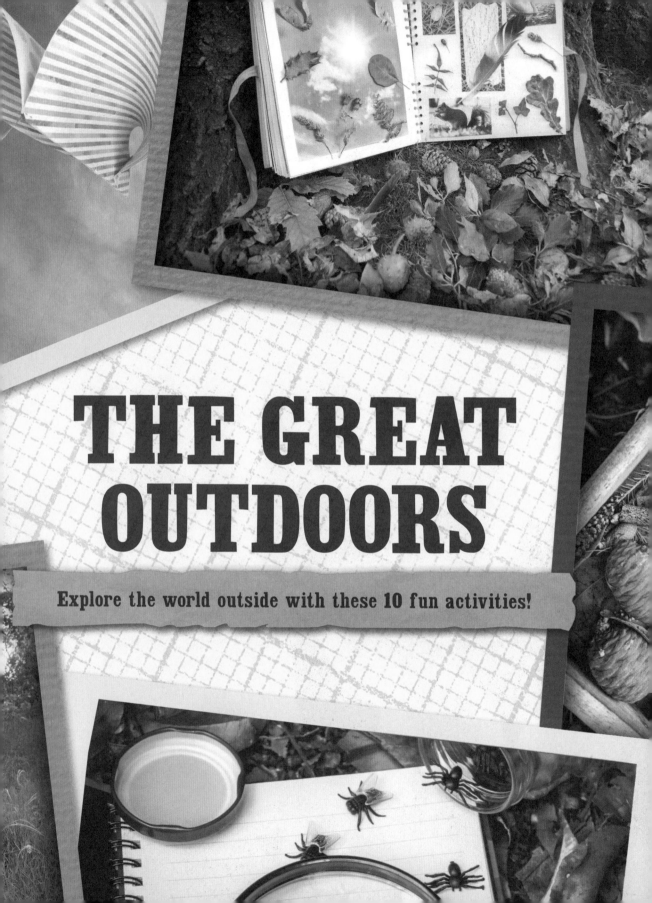

THE GREAT OUTDOORS

Explore the world outside with these **10** fun activities!

Build Your Own Bug Hotel

Make a simple bug hotel for attracting and observing creepy-crawly critters.

Children have a strange fascination with creepy-crawly insects. If it's slimy, hairy, and ugly, with wiggly antennae, 88 legs, and 13 boggling eyes, chances are they'll want it as a pet. Creating a bug hotel is a great way for your child to get hands-on with insects, while also giving the nature in your yard a helping hand to survive. It couldn't be easier or cheaper to create a bug hotel. You can use all kinds of scraps (see the "You will need" section below)—and any natural plant life that's lying around your yard is fantastic for creating the equivalent of a five-star hotel. Insects, such as beetles, spiders, ladybugs, and bumblebees, will love it. So get creative and don't limit yourself to our suggestions—some people even stuff pieces of old bricks and their old smelly socks in their bug hotels. Get as creative as you want, every bug hotel is unique.

You will need:

- old flowerpot (or more if you like)
- a selection of bug-friendly materials, such as grass cuttings, dead wood, hay, straw, leaves, sticks, bark, cones, and other organic matter, stones, parts of brick, and old tiles
- magnifying glass
- wood pallets or logs (optional)
- bricks (optional)

DAD TIP

Use a well-hidden video camera or webcam to spy on bug activity when you're not around, so you can keep an eye on your hotel's guests.

GETTING STARTED

Work with your child to create your own custom-made bug hotel. Turn your flowerpot on its side, so the bugs will be able to crawl in and out easily. Start stuffing your odd pieces inside the pot, keeping the heavy things toward the back and filling in the gaps with lighter items, such as straw or dead leaves. "Snug as a bug" is not just an old saying—insects genuinely do like cramped spaces, so make sure you squash as much as possible in there. Sections of old bamboo canes make a great resting place for bees, while fresh plant leaves and grass cuttings make great nests for hibernating bugs. Spiders, centipedes, and ladybugs love bark chippings, while bigger insects, such as beetles and wood lice, will be attracted to twigs. Try to find dry leaves to stuff in there, too, if possible, because these mimic the forest floor and will bring in a host of bugs looking for a cozy place to rest. You can never squash enough into your flowerpot, so go for it. It's good to use things from your local environment, because this will attract bugs from that same environment.

BRING ON THE BUGS

To make sure your bug hotel gets a lot of reservations from creepy-crawly guests, you need to find the right location for your completed hotel. Most insects do not like wind, so try to find a sheltered spot for your bug hotel flowerpot. Although many of the bugs might like it damp, you don't want a completely soggy hotel or the insides of your flowerpot might wash away, so try to find a spot in your yard that won't get too wet if it rains.

Direct sunlight is not ideal for many insects, such as earwigs and wood lice, which will find it unbearable; chances are, you won't have any guests other than bees (who love the sunshine). However, get the right spot and you will be amazed how quickly your bug hotel fills up. There are insects hidden everywhere out there and, within a couple of hours, we are sure you will have guests checking into your hotel. Carefully observe them using your magnifying glass and, if business is slow, you could leave a little piece of rotting fruit at the front of your pot to drive the guests absolutely wild! You should expect to attract a whole range of bugs, such as bees, butterflies, wasps, wood lice, ladybugs, along with spiders and a few slugs and snails—and even maybe some amphibians, such as frogs.

CREATE A BUG MANSION

If you've got space in your yard, you could build a larger, more elaborate version of a bug hotel. Use wooden pallets or logs to build layers or floors of the hotel, with bricks placed between layers for support. Leave small spaces between the wood panels to stuff with the natural materials to attract the bugs and drill holes in the logs to allow insects to crawl inside. If you place different types of material in the various spaces, you will attract different bugs to different "rooms." Make sure that the construction is well-supported and weighed down with enough stones and bricks to make sure it survives all winds and weathers.

DAD TIP

If you don't have a flowerpot, an old shoe box works just as well.

DAD TIP

Spring is the best time for getting a superbusy bug hotel, but you can attract bugs at any time of the year.

Build Your Own Natural Shelter

Make a natural shelter in the middle of the great outdoors.

There is perhaps no better way to while away the hours outdoors than by building a good old-fashioned shelter. Your child will love playing in their own space that you've created together.

You can build one almost anywhere—from deep within a nearby forest or woods to under a small gathering of trees in your local park. All you need to do is master how to make a simple frame out of wood. Once you've built your shelter, you and your child can use it to play in, to observe local wildlife from, or even to camp in if you're feeling extremely brave and adventurous (see page 38). However, remember to dismantle your shelter and scatter any natural materials back where you found them, because they will become important habitats for local insects and wildlife.

This project shows you how to build a simple three-pole shelter, but you can make your shelter as large or as small as you like. If you require a bigger A-frame shelter, just use additional shorter poles and line them up along the length of the longer pole.

You will need:
- long branch or pole (slightly longer than you are tall)
- two short poles (around half your height)
- branches and twigs of varying lengths
- leaves and forest debris
- rope
- knife
- waterproof tarpaulin or cover (optional)

DAD TIP

Don't use branches or logs any thicker than your wrist to cover your frame, because they may be too heavy for the frame to support.

GETTING STARTED

First of all, you need to choose your site. If you get the right location, with all the materials close by, building your shelter will be much simpler and quicker to construct. You could be warm, dry, and ready to use your shelter in under an hour. So, look for an area that has plenty of fallen branches and fallen leaves. Find an area of flat ground without too many lumps and bumps, so it will be more comfortable to sleep on. Remember to check for any insect nests, such as ants' and wasps' nests, before you start building, and check you aren't building over any burrows. Have a look above you to see if you are underneath any hanging or dead branches that could fall onto your shelter. Finally, stay out of any hollows or holes, because these will become puddles when it rains.

If you don't want to be too far away from home, you can also build an outdoor shelter in your own backyard. You might need to go to a local park or woodland, however, to source the materials before creating your shelter if you don't have everything readily available in your own yard.

THE BUILD

Once you've found the ideal spot to place your shelter, you can start to build.

1) Look for the poles in the form of fallen branches—try finding ones that have natural bends at the ends that will hook together and keep the frame more rigid.

2) Make the shape of an upside-down "V" with your two short poles. Securely tie the poles together at the top end where they cross over.

3) Place one end of the long pole across the join of the two shorter poles. Prop the other end of the long pole on the ground so that the structure is balanced and steady, like a tripod. Securely tie the longer pole to the upside-down "V" poles so all three poles are tied together. The two shorter poles should be upright, with the longer pole as a prop to steady it.

4) If you want a larger, more substantial A-frame shelter, you can tie more upside-down "V"-shape poles along the whole length of the long pole instead of resting the longer pole on the ground. This will create a steadier and larger structure.

5) Next, fill the space between the ground and the long pole with plenty of branches and sticks. At first, use larger branches that you can trim to exactly fit the space, then fill in any gaps with smaller twigs. Make sure the branches and twigs don't stick up above the long pole if you want your shelter to be waterproof.

6) Now, gather handfuls of leaves and forest debris and use them to cover the frame. Start by covering the bottom of the shelter all the way around and then keep going from the bottom up to the long pole. You will then need about a 4-inch/10-cm deep covering if you want to keep the rain out.

7) If you are camping and want a guaranteed waterproof shelter, place a light tarpaulin or waterproof covering over the frame as well for added peace of mind.

DAD TIP

Never use mosses, ferns, or wild flowers to cover your shelter, because they may be rare or even a protected species.

DAD TIP

Never break branches from a living tree, because this could let infection in and possibly even kill the tree.

How to Build a Campfire

Making a campfire can be loads of fun if done properly and safely.

⚠ Safety alert! Be especially careful with this activity—fires need to be prepared and tended extremely carefully. Children need to be monitored at all times and kept at a safe distance from the fire. However, once you've got your "Safety Dad" mode on, go for it, because campfires are plenty of fun. Sitting by a campfire is a truly satisfying and rewarding experience, and showing your child how to prepare and light a campfire only adds to the enjoyment.

First of all, before you start, you need to check the local regulations in the area where you plan to have a campfire. Regulations vary by state, with some being more strict than others, especially in the states where wild fires are a serious risk. If you are planning to camp in a national forest, you may still need a state permit—for example, if camping in Sequoia National Forest, make sure you have a California campfire permit (which is also needed for barbecues). Regulations may also be different within certain areas of a park, forest, or even beach. If you are going camping and were hoping to have a campfire, first check online, because restrictions may also be temporary, depending on current weather conditions. So check first, then get going.

You will need:

- shovel
- stones
- pail of water or fire extinguisher
- tinder, kindling, and dry fuel wood (see the "Gather your Equipment" section)
- lighter or matches

PREPARING THE SITE

Preparation is key. Making several attempts or lighting your fire only to watch it smolder and die out is a frustrating and demoralizing activity. So think carefully about where to site your fire. If you are camping, always position a campfire downwind of where you want to sit or pitch your tent. Choose a large, open area so that you can move freely around your campfire, and keep well away from overhanging branches, grassland, or areas littered with dead leaves. Stony ground is perfect. Clear away any loose gravel, leaf debris, or pine needles, and remove any turf with your hands or a shovel. Your cleared area should be at least twice the size of your planned fire; this also creates the "no-go" area around the fire.

SAFETY FIRST

⚠ While you are lighting the fire, you need to keep your child away from the area and outside the "no-go" area. You should place a ring of stones around the "no-go" area so it is clear how close your child can get. Either get another adult to entertain your child, or keep your child at a safe distance to observe what's going on but with strict instructions not to come within the "no-go" area.

Do not create a campfire in extremely windy conditions and do not build your fire on an upward slope, because fire can spread quickly uphill. Always keep a pail of cold water or fire extinguisher handy so you can extinguish the fire quickly.

GATHER YOUR EQUIPMENT

If you build your fire properly, it should light the first time, every time. Gather your tinder, kindling, and dry fuel wood; your child will enjoy hunting the local area with you and helping to gather suitable fuel. For tinder, you will need something that lights easily to start your fire. This could be some birch or cherry-tree bark, a ball of dry grass, screwed-up newspaper, or even some cotton balls or sawdust. Next you'll need kindling; it should be twigs as thin as matchsticks, gathered into two fist-thick bundles.

You will also need some thicker sticks, about as thick as your thumb; these will be the fuel wood for your fire. You will also need a thick stick, about as thick as your wrist, to rest your kindling on. This will allow air to get into the fire.

BUILD IT UP

Lay down a flat bed of the fuel-wood sticks in the center of your fire site. It will stop moisture from the ground turning to steam and putting your fire out. Place the thick stick at one end of the bed. Place the tinder on the bed of fuel-wood sticks about 2 inches/5 cm from the thick stick and …

⚠ LIGHT IT UP!

Once you've lit your tinder, take a bundle of your kindling and place it over the flame, resting one end of the bundle on the thick stick and the other end of the bundle on the bed of sticks. Do the same thing with a second bundle of kindling. In an ideal world, you need your two bundles to cross each other above the flame. When the kindling begins to crackle, add some more, and when it really catches, you can add the thicker fuel wood as you want.

⚠ KEEP THE FIRE BURNING

When the fire is burning, never leave it unattended and keep your child closely monitored and outside the "no-go" area at all times. Keep your fire small, about as big as a basketball—do not let it grow. Make sure your child doesn't throw anything onto the fire.

⚠ PACKING UP

When you are ready to put out the fire, let it die out and make sure it is completely extinguished before leaving it unattended. Even once the flames have died out, the wood and ground will still be hot. Pour cold water over the site and stir up the area with a large stick until you are sure everything has completely gone out.

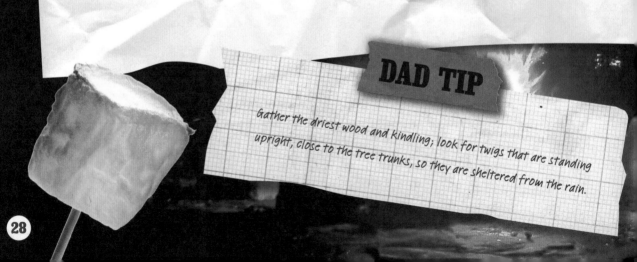

DAD TIP

Gather the driest wood and kindling; look for twigs that are standing upright, close to the tree trunks, so they are sheltered from the rain.

Collect wood from the local area, but remember to take only fallen branches. Do not remove any branches from standing trees.

Classic Glider

Have the best-looking glider in the park made from just a cereal box.

You will need:
- template from pages 122–123
- child-friendly scissors
- 1 large cereal box
- scrap piece of corrugated cardboard larger than the cereal box
- clear tape
- craft knife (optional)
- ruler
- ballpoint pen
- modeling clay
- paints and paintbrush, to decorate as you want (optional)

Step 1:
Photocopy the templates on pages 122—123 or trace around them. Cut the templates into smaller sections with scissors.

⏱ **Time to make:** about 15 minutes

Step 2:
Cut the cereal box along one of the seams and lay it out flat, with the printed side down, on top of a thick piece of corrugated cardboard to protect the work surface. Use small lengths of tape to secure the fuselage template to the cardboard, making sure the dotted center line is over a crease.

⚠ Use either a craft knife or scissors to carefully cut out the fuselage, cutting along all the scissor lines. It's important to be as accurate as possible when cutting out the glider, because any mistakes could prevent your glider from flying properly.

2.

Step 3:

Use small lengths of tape to secure the wings template in place, avoiding any creases in the box.

⚠ Carefully cut out the template along the scissor lines, using a craft knife or scissors and protecting the work surface with the corrugated cardboard.

Step 4:

Attach the tail template to the cardboard in the same way as the other parts. Using a ruler and a ballpoint pen, press hard and draw along the solid lines to create a crease in the cardboard. Don't press too hard to avoid tearing the cardboard.

Step 5:

⚠ Cut out the tail along the scissor lines.

Step 6:

Fold the fuselage in half with the printed side facing inward. Gently slide the wings into the two forward-facing slots in the middle. Curl the wings slightly and slide it into the slots at the nose end.

Step 7:

Slide the tail into the slots at the back end of the fuselage until it can go no farther.

Step 8:

Roll a marble-size amount of modeling clay (or use the guide on the template) into a ball. Squash it between your fingers and thumb to about the size of the larger guide on the template.

Step 9:

Place the modeling clay disk into the nose and gently squeeze the sides of the glider together so the clay sticks to at least one side. Use a piece of tape, about 1½ inches/4 cm long, to hold the two sides together. Decorate the glider with paints, if desired, especially underneath the wings and tail, the areas that will be seen when it flies.

DAD TIP

Throw the glider gently to start with. If the glider climbs and then quickly falls (called a stall), you will need to add a little more modeling clay to the nose. Add a small amount at a time and test the glider until it flies without stalling. If the glider nosedives into the ground, remove a small amount of modeling clay from the nose and test until it flies a good distance before landing smoothly. To make your glider do a loop, gently bend the ailerons (movable flaps) on the tail upward. The more you bend, the tighter the loop. Fly your glider on a calm day with only the gentlest of breezes, otherwise it will not fly properly and could be blown away and damaged. Throwing your glider into a gentle breeze will give the best results. It will fly farther and loop better. Do not attempt to fly on a rainy day.

Make Your Own Explorer Kit

Take a boring old suitcase or briefcase and turn it into an adventurer's tool kit, ready for any expedition.

You will need:

A small suitcase, briefcase, large lunch box, or empty tool kit with a handle, as well as equipment for your kit (see right).

A child's imagination needs a only little jump-start and it can create whole worlds out of practically nothing. A saucepan on the head is an astronaut's hat, a stick is a cowboy's gun, and a cardboard box is a knight's castle!

As a Dad, your child will be happy to take you on an adventure through their imagination with them—and making an explorer's kit can be a great first step into exploring that imagination together. By taking an old briefcase or suitcase and filling it with a few basic items, you can create something that will really get the imaginative juices flowing. It shouldn't take more than 15 minutes to create and it should be inexpensive to make. Once you have your kit, you and your child can go on wild adventures together. How about climbing the great mountain range that is a hill in your local park or exploring the jungle that is that untamed area of your backyard? Be as creative as you want to help fuel your child's inner mini-explorer.

FILL YOUR KIT!

There are a million different things you could fill your explorer kit with. Tailor the ideas below to something that you think will work for your child. Go through the list together and add any other ideas you come up with from around the home. Then fill your case until it's bursting at the seams ...

- Magnifying glass
- Binoculars
- String
- Compass
- Tape measure
- Map of your local area
- Camera
- Notepad
- Flashlight
- Jars with vented lids or bug-friendly jars
- Child-friendly scissors
- Candles (that you can pretend are SOS flares)
- Pens and pencils
- Creature-identifying book (for bugs, birds, or wildlife)
- Water pistol
- Telescope
- Watch
- Whistle
- Small fishing net
- Small shovel

PLACES TO EXPLORE

There are plenty of places you can take your child to explore—some good places are the yard, a nearby park or forest, or a river or pond close by. Woods and forests are magical places for children; there are so many unfamiliar sights and sounds and it feels like you're just one wrong footstep from entering a Grimm's fairy tale.

BECOME AN EXPLORER

There are a number of ways that you and your child can have fun exploring. Below are just a few suggestions for explorer games.

BUG EXPLORER

Explore any local greenery armed with your magnifying glass and some bug jars. You can dig for worms or collect some bugs from flowers or under rocks. For older children, bring along a bug-identification book and get them to look up which bugs they've discovered. Once the bugs have been discovered, capture the creepy-crawly critters in the bug jars and get your child to draw a sketch in their notebook. Before you go, release the bugs back into their natural environment.

UNDERWATER EXPLORER

Ponds and rivers are filled with interesting wildlife that your child will want to explore. Using jars filled with pond water and a small fishing net, children can investigate any creatures they find, such as tadpoles, bugs, snails, and small fish. Take along a water creature identification guide to help educate older children about what they find. Children will need to be accompanied at all times when by the water.

ANIMAL TRACKER EXPLORER

Encourage your child to find out about the secret life of animals by exploring their tracks. In your yard, place a folded white sheet in an area where you think animals might visit. Place some food, such as fruit or vegetable scraps, in the middle of the sheet, then sprinkle some fresh soil around all the edges of the sheet. Weigh the sheet down at the corners with stones. Before nightfall, thoroughly wet the sheet and the soil with water. Your children will be very excited to wake up the next morning to see if any tracks have

DAD TIP

Make sure that your child doesn't damage any of the wildlife during their explorations to encourage a positive relationship with nature.

DAD TIP

If you don't have a suitable map of the local area, draw one with an "X marks the spot" for the treasure. Maps can be made to look old by carefully baking the paper in a low oven.

appeared. You can have plenty of fun identifying the tracks and moving the sheet around the yard to see if different tracks appear.

TREASURE HUNTER EXPLORER

For children who are less interested in nature, you can use the explorer kit for a good old-fashioned treasure hunt. You can have a pirate theme with dressing up or get them to pretend to be famous explorers for a more educational game. For younger children, you might want to have the treasure hunt at home, but older children might want to explore the park with you. Bury the treasure (either literally in a shallow hole or crevice or hide it). Then create the clues—picture clues are best for younger children, with riddles or cryptic clues for older children. Increase the difficulty of the clues as the game progresses. Using your explorer kit, get them to go in a certain direction using their compass, or give them a map to find their way to specific clues. You could also place things at certain distances and get them to measure with their tape measure or mention small or high-up details that they need to use their binoculars to spot.

A Backyard Campout

Going on vacation to an official campsite can be fun, but your tent doesn't have to sit in a closet gathering dust when you're not on vacation. So why not get out that tent and camp out in the backyard with your child? It's a simple way to turn a normal night into an exciting adventure. Your child will love the novelty of sleeping so close yet so far from home and, most important of all, it provides a great opportunity to have time away from the distractions of television and computer games indoors. What's more, in your own private backyard campsite, there are no boring rules and regulations, no campsite charges, and hopefully no noisy neighbors.

You will need:
- tent
- bedding
- pajamas
- flashlight
- telescope or binoculars (optional)
- some musical instruments
- string
- two metal cans
- screwdriver
- balloons
- football
- apples
- pail
- yard decorations (optional)

HOW TO MAKE YOUR CAMPOUT EXTRA SPECIAL

PITCHING THE TENT

You could try making the outdoor shelter from page 22 or just put up your own tent. Your child will enjoy getting all the tent parts laid out and fitted together, while you hammer in the pegs at the end.

Start your campout fun by gathering together all the bedding and nightwear from your house and taking it out to the tent. Get your child to select sleeping positions and set up their bedding for the night ahead.

DECORATE THE YARD

You don't have to go crazy, but a few simple decorations could add some atmosphere to your backyard. Try putting a few tea lights in jars around the yard or put up some simple flags between trees and bushes.

TRY SOME OUTDOOR GAMES

Before nightfall, play football, charades, catch, tag, apple bobbing, or hide-and-seek. Make sure that everyone has had a really good chance to run around so that the chance of them actually falling asleep is much higher.

HAVE WATER-BOMB FUN

Balloons filled with water can bring the laughter to a backyard campsite, particularly on a really hot summer evening. And remember, if things get too silly, you can just run back into the safety of your home to dry off.

TALK ON METAL-CAN TELEPHONES

By connecting two cans to a piece of string, you can make an old-school telephone to talk from one end of the yard to the other. Dad should create a hole in the bottom of each can, using a screwdriver, drill, or hammer, and tie a string between the cans.

STARGAZE

If you've got a telescope or binoculars, bring them, but on a clear night you can really enjoy the stars even with the naked eye. See what constellations you can spot or try to find the

International Space Station. Draw maps of the stars you can see and make up names to remember them by for the next time you adventure in the great outdoors.

GO NOCTURNAL ANIMAL SPOTTING

Try to spot signs of the animals that come out only at night. Listen for owls, raccoons, opossums, foxes, badgers, and more. If you have a pet cat, you'll probably be amazed at how active they are once darkness falls in your yard.

SING SOME SONGS

You might feel silly at first, but once the songs get going, you'll have fun. And don't just stick to the classic campout songs. Who needs "Kumbaya" or "Old MacDonald," when the camp can be rocked with a little "Bohemian Rhapsody" or some One Direction?

TELL STORIES

If your children are young or particularly sensitive, you might want to avoid ghost stories and just do some simple storytelling games. Come up with an opening sentence to a story and then get the child to continue the tale in an imaginative way. Examples could be "When the aliens invaded earth…" or "The wizard had just discovered a new special power…" For older children, have fun with ghost stories. Place a flashlight under your face and share some scary tales. Obviously, don't make them so scary that your children want to run away and hide back in your home. Always try to keep your ghost stories lighthearted so that your children know that they're just some fun and not something to have nightmares over.

MAKE HAND SHADOWS

All you need is a flashlight and the canvas of your tent. Anybody can do a rabbit, but see if you can shape your hands to make a duck, a rooster, a bear, and a butterfly.

DAD TIP

You can create the outdoor shelter that is described on page 22 during the daytime if you want a whole day of outdoor fun.

DAD TIP

If your children are young, bring their teddy bears outside for the campout; it will make the adventure all the more magic.

We're Going on a Scavenger Hunt

Head outside to search in your yard and beyond...

A scavenger hunt is a great way to let kids safely explore their local environment while having some real fun. It couldn't be easier—all you need is to create a list of items to scavenge for and then head outside. People get confused between a treasure hunt and a scavenger hunt, but there is a difference. Treasure hunts involve following clues to find hidden treasure, whereas a scavenger hunt involves finding a list of items within a certain time frame.

The trick is to get really hands-on with the nature around you as you hunt and encourage your child to do the same. Touch, sight, smell, sound, get all your child's senses going, as you collect a bounty of pinecones, snail shells, feathers, wildflowers, and more.

It doesn't matter whether you live in the country or in the heart of a busy town or city, because there's often nature lurking wherever you are. Make the hunt as exciting as it is educational by rummaging around looking for secrets hiding in shrubs, under rocks, and among the greenery of your neighborhood. Just follow these simple steps and get on the scavenger hunt trail!

Remember that if you have more than one child doing the hunt, you will need to make sure they do the activity as a team so you can carefully supervise everyone, or take along a few other adults.

You will need:

- pencil
- paper
- wax crayons
- jar
- tape measure
- camera phone or camera

CREATE YOUR CHECKLIST

Before you head out, draw a grid on a piece of 8½ x 11-inch/ 21 x 28-cm paper with three horizontal lines (3 inches/7.5 cm apart) and two vertical lines (3 inches/7.5 cm apart). This will give you 12 boxes to fill with the following ideas. Write each one in the space of the box, perhaps drawing a little illustration of each of the highlighted words to help the list really come to life for your little one:

• Collect some **grass** and soil in your jar
• Make a bark rubbing from a **tree** with your crayons
• Find an animal's **footprint** or tracks
• Collect a **feather**
• Hear a **bird** song, then try to whistle or sing it
• Smell a **wildflower**
• Find a **snail**'s shell
• Look for a **bird**'s nest in a tree
• Collect a **pinecone**
• Capture a **bug** in your jar
• Count the rings on a **tree stump**
• Find and feel a shiny, smooth **stone**.

For slightly older children, you might want to replace some of the items with the following more challenging suggestions:

• Find a twig shaped like a "Y"
• Draw something beginning with "B" that you see
• Take a peek inside an animal's burrow
• Use a tape measure to measure the width of a tree trunk
• Find an item that you can recycle
• Take a photo of your reflection in some water.

DAD TIP

Why not turn the pinecone you collect into a bird feeder when you get home? Simply tie a ribbon to the pinecone, cover it in peanut butter, and hang it from a tree. Birds cannot resist.

DAD TIP

Squeamish? If you hate the thought of a jar full of bugs, why not take your camera out? Getting your child to take a photo of an insect can be as much fun as putting Mr. Bug in a jar.

HEAD OUTSIDE AND HAVE SOME FUN

Got the list? Well come on then, let's go. As Dads, it's up to us to take a little control of directions, so your child doesn't just wander aimlessly. Keeping your child's interest is a high priority and they will easily become frustrated if they can't find at least one or two things quickly. So think about where you're going and gently lead your child to a place where they can easily cross off a couple of boxes.

To give the hunt some focus, it is a good idea to set a time limit for finding the items. For older children, this can be short because they will find it fun to run around and find all the items.

Obviously, make sure you don't trespass into people's yards, look out for poison ivy, dog mess, and litter, and remember that some places don't let you pick wildflowers.

Essentially, you just need to head out and treat your scavenger hunt like a big outdoor game of bingo. Cross each item off your list as you find or do them, and a full house wins. If there's more than one child, have a checklist for each child and perhaps include a prize for whoever can find every item or the most items. But make sure not to lose anyone while you keep the contest going.

DAD TIP

A scavenger hunt is a great way to encourage recycling. If you find a lot of litter on your search, use a plastic bag and show your child how people who love nature deal with waste.

WHY NOT?

Use some of the items from your scavenger hunt in a nature scrapbook (see page 46).

Create a Nature Scrapbook

Scrapbooking is a great way to get your kids into being creative, while preserving some memories at the same time.

You will need:

- spiral- or ring-bound scrapbook with thick paper
- nature image printouts
- crayons
- glue stick or clear tape
- felt-tip pens
- colored pencils
- child-friendly scissors
- old newspapers and magazines
- glitter
- transparent adhesive vinyl
- sheets of 8½ x 11-inch/ 21 x 28-cm paper
- materials collected on walks, such as photos, dried leaves, twigs, feathers, dried flowers, etc.

The first rule of scrapbooking is that there are no rules of scrapbooking. The second rule of scrapbooking is there ... are ... no ... rules of scrapbooking. A scrapbook can be whatever you want it to be—just get involved and fill it with leaves, bark rubbings, photos, anything and everything.

The key is to get a good scrapbook to start with. You will be filling this scrapbook with glue, photographs, clear tape, and more, so invest in something that at least feels like it isn't going to fall apart at the first sight of a glue stick. It is probably a good idea to get a spiral- or ring-bound scrapbook, because the pages will be easiesr to lay out flat as you and your child work on the pages.

You can put together your scrapbook however you want, but here are some suggestions for how you could fill the pages.

CREATE A BACKGROUND

To start off your nature scrapbook, you will need to create backgrounds for the pages. You can either get your child to print off a large image that you have found together online—images that make good backdrops include grass, sunsets, the sky. Or you could get your child to draw a background, using crayons to draw images of flowers, grass, etc., to cover the page. You can create different backgrounds for each page and you can either do all the backgrounds at once or do them as you create each page.

STICK IN SOME PHOTOGRAPHS

To add to your nature scrapbook, a good place to start is with a good assortment of photographs of things you have seen on your adventures. Get your child to try their luck at nature photography and see if they can snap any local wildlife in action. To give them a helping hand, take feed to bribe local ducks with or carrots for horses that you know live nearby. Squirrels will sometimes pose for photographs if you have some peanuts to tempt them with. Once the photographs are printed, get your child to cut them out carefully and stick them into the scrapbook. You can either use photograph corners or just glue them straight onto the page. Ask your child to annotate each photograph with entertaining captions of what the image is, where it was taken, and why they like the picture.

MAKE A NATURE COLLAGE

Not all the photos have to be your own. Find some old magazines and newspapers and cut out any pictures you see of wildlife, rivers, and plants that your child likes. Get them to paste them into your scrapbook, label each picture, and add decoration, such as glitter, to bring the pages to life.

DAD TIP

When gluing things down, avoid placing glue in the center, because it can warp the surface and create craters on your page.

ADD REAL PLANTS

A great way to preserve and display all the dried leaves, twigs, dried flowers, and feathers you have collected on your scavenger hunt (see page 42) is with a collage for your scrapbook. To do this you will need two sheets of transparent adhesive vinyl—you will need to help your child if they find this difficult. Tape the nonsticky side of a sheet to a table, so the sticky side is facing up. Then place all of the nature goodies you want to display onto the sheet. After that, remove the tape and stick a second sheet on top, sticky side up, then turn it over and press it firmly down into your scrapbook.

ADD A JOURNAL OR POEM

On a separate sheet of paper, get your child to write down what they particularly love about a certain aspect of nature. If they can't think of something off the top of their head, help them out and suggest they write about what they would do if they ever saw a grizzly bear in their yard. Cut this out and glue it down.

ADD SKETCHES AND RUBBINGS

Fill your scrapbook with sketches of the insects you catch each night in your bug hotel (see page 18). Make bark rubbings by placing a sheet of paper over the top of a tree bark and rubbing it with a crayon.

CREATE THEMED PAGES

A good way to keep your child's interest in a nature scrapbook is to get them to introduce themes to the pages. Some suggestions are: My favorite flowers; My favorite things in the park; My favorite things in the yard; Animals I would like to see in real life; My favorite nature facts. Encourage your child to be creative—get them to use a variety of colors and textures and to use a mixture of words and images.

DAD TIP

If you have access to a photocopier, it's a great way of keeping your original photographs safe from glue!

Let's Go Fly a Kite

This is an incredibly easy kite to make and it can be decorated with your own designs.

You will need:

- 1 sheet of 11 x 14-inch/ 28 x 35-cm paper
- ruler
- pencil
- stapler
- hole punch
- 32-inch/80-cm-long thin ribbon
- 24-inch/60-cm-long wide ribbon
- scissors
- ball of thin string
- felt-tip pens, crayons, or paints, to decorate as you want

Time to make: about 30 minutes

Step 1:

Take a sheet of 11 x 14-inch/28 x 35-cm paper in a color of your choice and decorate it with felt-tip pens and crayons on both sides. Fold the paper in half widthwise, making sure the shortest edges meet at the top.

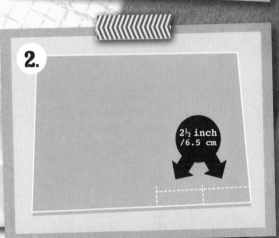

Step 2:

With the creased edge at the bottom, facing toward you, measure 2½ inches/6.5 cm from the right-hand edge and mark this with a pencil. Measure another 2½ inches/6.5 cm from the first pencil mark and mark again with a pencil.

2½ inch /6.5 cm

Step 3:

With the creased edge at the bottom, curl over the top layer of paper so that the top right-hand corner meets the first pencil mark. Hold it in place with your finger.

Step 4:

Pick up the paper, still holding the first corner in place, and curl over the other side to meet the same pencil mark. Pinch together between finger and thumb and staple the two sides together, making sure not to catch your fingers in the stapler.

Step 5:

Use a hole punch to punch a hole at the second pencil mark. Be careful not to punch the hole too close to the edge of the paper.

Step 6:

With a ruler and pencil, take one end of the thin ribbon and make six marks at 4-inch/10-cm intervals along the length of the ribbon. There should still be an unmarked length of 8 inches/20 cm at the end.

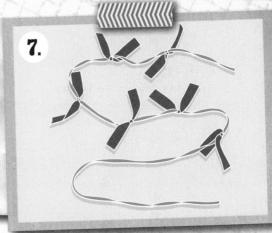

6.

Step 7:

⚠ Cut the wide ribbon into six shorter lengths, each measuring 4 inches/10 cm. Tie these short ribbons around the thin ribbon in a small knot at each of the marked intervals.

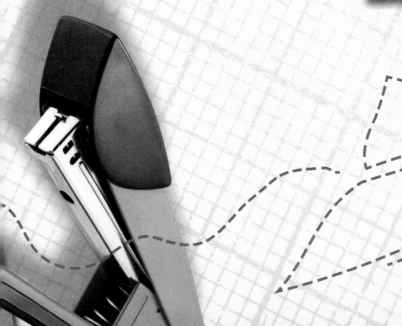

7.

Step 8:

Use the stapler to staple one end of the thin ribbon to the opposite end of the creased fold.

Step 9:

Thread the string through the hole you created with the hole punch. Tie the string in a loose loop (not too tight otherwise the string will cut the paper).

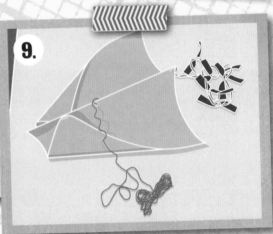

Step 10:

It's time to fly your kite. You'll need a good breeze, but not too windy or your kite might just blow away.

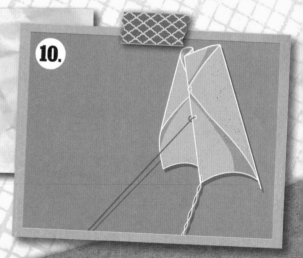

DAD TIP

Make sure to decorate the underside of the kite, because this is what will show when you fly it.

A Day at the Beach

Skipping stones and collecting as many shiny seashells as your pockets will hold, the beach is a special place for Dad and child.

Close your eyes. Think of a great day out from your own childhood. Chances are you just saw the golden sand of a beach, ice creams melting as fast as you could eat them, and noisy seagulls all playing out to a soundtrack of roaring waves. Yes, the seashore dominates so many of our great childhood memories and the beach really can be such a magical place for children. To make a day out at the coast extra special, it can be a great idea to pack in some really fun activities, such as beachcombing, searching tide pools, sand building, or fossil hunting. Here are some ideas on how to turn a day at the seashore with Dad into memories that will last forever.

You will need:
- pail
- shovel
- waterproof nonslip footwear
- plastic containers
- small fishing net
- fossil-identification guide
- empty beverage bottles
- scissors

GO BEACHCOMBING

From coins to shells to lost pails and shovels, there's a whole bounty of hidden treasure buried just underneath the sand. Beachcombing is like the ultimate treasure hunt, so simply start exploring. Dig through the sand, sift it with your fingers or with a small-mesh fishing net, and fill a plastic container with what you find. This is best done at the coastline during a low or receding tide or right after a storm, because this is when you find the most treasures. Once you're done, why not take your treasure home? Pebbles, shells, driftwood, and feathers all make wonderful things to paint on a rainy day when you wish you were still by the sea.

EXPLORE A TIDE POOL

For successful exploring of a tide pool, search for rocky areas on sandy or stony seashores that are fairly sheltered. Other sheltered areas, such as underneath piers, can also provide good places for finding marine life. It is best to go at low tide; consult a tide chart and head to the area about 30 minutes before low tide so you have plenty of time for collecting. Carefully look under rocks and in pools, using a plastic container filled with seawater to collect any creatures. Make sure you change the water regularly and keep different creatures separate to avoid fighting. Respect the marine life; you should never kill or take a live animal with you. Carefully supervise your child at all time. Remember that some creatures have claws, and rocks can be slippery, so waterproof shoes with good grip are essential.

FOSSIL HUNTING

Beaches are great places for you and your children to find fossils. You can find fossils either along the coastline or among clusters of rocks. Sandy areas, close to where the tide has just gone out, are a good place to start looking. Do a little online research before

DAD TIP

Sturdy, waterproof footwear is essential when climbing on rocks, because they can be slippery and potentially sharp.

you head out to see what fossils might be in your region and where might be the best spot to find them. Depending on where you're looking, you could find the fossils of ancient sponges or pollen grains, dinosaur footprints, bones, shark teeth, snails, fish, and more. Take along a pail or plastic container to collect your finds. You could bring a fossil-identification guide with you or research when you get home to discover what kinds of fossils you have found. As with searching tide pools, careful supervision and sturdy shoes are essential.

BUILD A SAND MAN

We've all built sand castles, but why not branch out and build a sand man? A sand man looks like a snowman, but, obviously, is made out of wet sand. Make three balls out of wet sand: a large, medium, and small ball. Place the medium ball on top of the larger ball, then add the small ball on top. Decorate the sand man, using pebbles for eyes and a mouth, a twig or driftwood for a nose and arms, and seaweed for hair.

MAKE A NATURAL WADING POOL

A quick-and-easy way to have fun on the beach is to dig out a wading pool in the sand. All you need is a pail and shovel and the energy to dig. Start digging out a small, circular hole, a short distance from the sea. The hole should be wide enough for your child to stand and easily move around in. Place the sand that you dig out around the edge of the circle so that it forms a natural wall around the edge of your pool. Dig down until you hit water and fill the pool slightly with more water from a pail until you have enough water for your child to wade in. Don't dig down too deep. Your child should only be up to their knees in the hole when standing up, so go nearer to the sea if you have to dig deeper before you hit water.

MAKE A SAND-CASTLE WATER FOUNTAIN

Help your child to build a sand castle that becomes a really impressive water fountain.

Step 1:

⚠ Collect a few empty beverage bottles. Clean them out, remove the labels, and screw the lids on. Cut each bottle in half, straight across the middle, using sharp scissors. Both halves are going to act like little "pails" to hold the water.

Step 2:

⚠ Using scissors or another sharp implement, make two small holes near the bottom of each pail, about 2 inches/5 cm up from the bottom and at least 1 inch/2.5 cm apart from each other.

Step 3:

Build a large sand castle, piled high into the shape of a mountain. Place a pail at the top of the sand castle, burying the bottom securely into the sand but making sure the holes are kept clear. Then place two pails below the holes of the top pail, so that the water will cascade out of each hole into the open tops of the two pails below. Arrange all the other pails down the sand castle so that the water flows from one pail to another, all the way down to the bottom of the sand castle.

Step 4:

Get your child to collect some seawater and pour the water into the pail at the top. Watch the water cascade down all the pails to the bottom. Your child will have plenty of fun filling up the fountain with seawater again and again. And there's no limit to how big and intricate you can make the arrangement of the fountain.

DAD TIP

Sea glass can be taken home to make a great mosaic. It's usually safe for children, because the ocean wears away any sharp edges, but check before giving to your child.

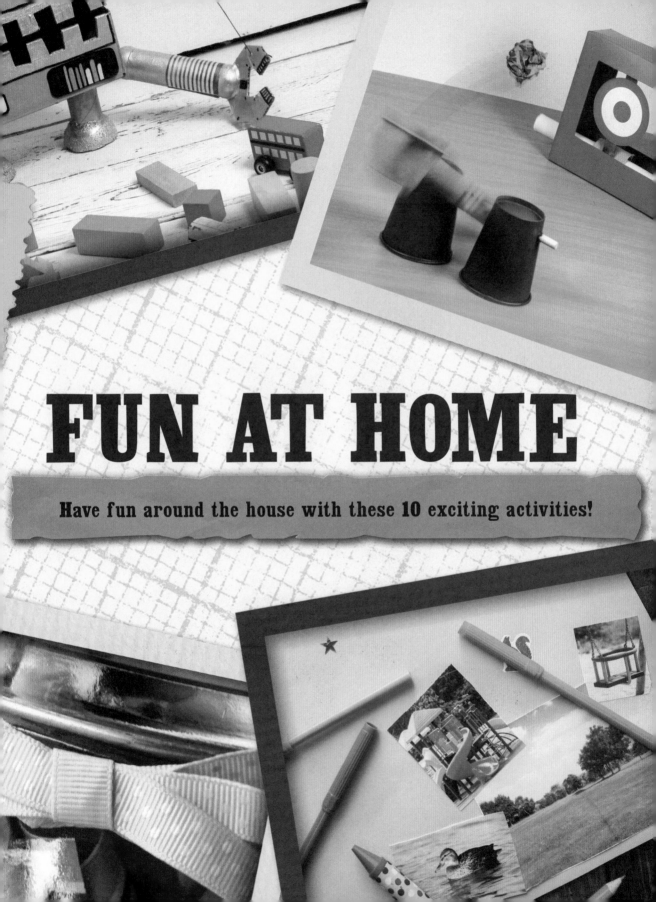

FUN AT HOME

Have fun around the house with these **10** exciting activities!

Drawbridge Castle

This castle, with its own working drawbridge, will be the talk of the town. Just add a princess or a knight in shining armor to bring it to life.

You will need:

- 1 large, square thick corrugated cardboard box
- glue gun and glue sticks
- white craft glue
- packaging tape
- utility knife
- scissors
- marker pen
- ruler
- 2 large wooden craft/ ice pop sticks
- ballpoint pen
- 2 lengths (about 4 feet 11 inches/1.5 m) of packaging string
- 1 large ¾-inch/2-cm wooden bead
- 2 large, rectangular thick corrugated cardboard boxes
- 2 large mailing tubes
- 1 length (about 6 feet 6 inches/ 2 m) of thick ribbon
- colored cardstock
- stapler
- paints and paintbrush, to decorate as you want (optional)

DAD TIP

You can use any size of box for this project, depending on what is available and how big you want the castle to be. Thick, strong cardboard boxes like those used for storage would be ideal. As an indicator, the boxes for the tall towers need to be as high as just below the chin of the child you are making it for.

 Time to make:
1 hour

Step 1:

⚠️ Glue the bottom of the square cardboard box closed with a glue gun. Hold the flaps in place with packaging tape for extra support while the glue sets.

Step 2:

⚠️ Turn the box on its side and cut off one flap from the open end with a utility knife or scissors, then cut off the opposite side flap to leave only two flaps that are opposite each other.

Step 3:

Using a marker pen, draw the shape of a drawbridge on one side of the box that still has a flap attached. Leave a border on both sides of the drawbridge instead of making it the full width of the box.

⚠️ Cut out the shape using a utility knife, but be sure the drawbridge is still attached along the bottom edge so that it's hinged.

Step 4:

Draw three evenly spaced squares with a marker pen and ruler to meet the top edge on one of the flaps as a guide for cutting out castellations.

⚠ Cut out the squares with a utility knife and repeat on the other flap. Keep the squares you cut out to use later.

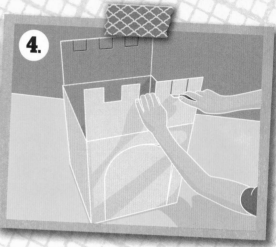

Step 5:

Turn the box over so that the side with the drawbridge is on the floor. Draw an arch on top of the box, making it big enough for your child to crawl through.

⚠ Cut out the arch with a utility knife, removing it completely, because it doesn't need to hinge. Keep the cutout from the arch to use later.

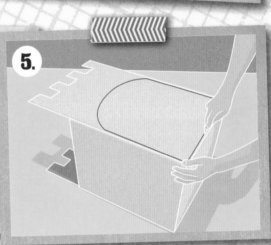

Step 6:

⚠ Glue two wooden craft/ice pop sticks to the top of the drawbridge door at a 45-degree angle and half covering the top of the curved entrance. Carefully push a ballpoint pen into the box above the entrance, behind the sticks, to create two holes that will be covered by the sticks when the drawbridge is closed. Tie one of the lengths of packaging string around one stick. Repeat with the other length of string on the second stick.

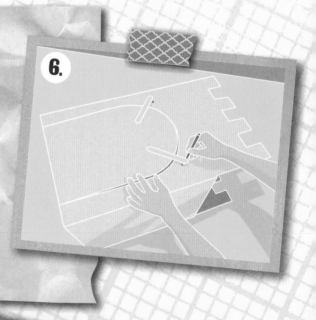

Step 7:

Push the ends of the string through the holes to the inside of the box and through the hole in the wooden bead. With the drawbridge completely open, slide the bead down the string until the string is taut. Tie the two loose ends together as close to the bead as you can get and trim the ⚠ excess string with a pair of scissors. Pull the strings to raise the drawbridge, then slide the bead up the string to hold the drawbridge closed.

Step 8:

⚠ To make a tower, glue down the bottom flaps of one of the rectangular boxes with hot glue, holding the flaps in place with packaging tape while the glue sets. Turn the box so the open flaps are at the top. Draw three evenly spaced squares with a marker pen and ruler to meet the top edge of one of the flaps as a guide for cutting out castellations.

Cut out the squares with a utility knife and repeat on the other flaps. Again, keep the little squares you cut out to use later.

Step 9:

Decide which side will be the back of the tower. Use the piece of arch-shaped cardboard, reserved from step 5, as a template to draw around and cut another arch from the back of this box.

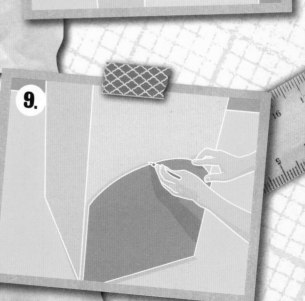

Step 10:

Remove the ends from the packaging tubes and mark a line about halfway down one of them. Draw two parallel lines, about 2 inches/5 cm apart, down to the end of the tube from this mark. ⚠ Carefully cut out this section using a utility knife. Be careful because the tube is tough.

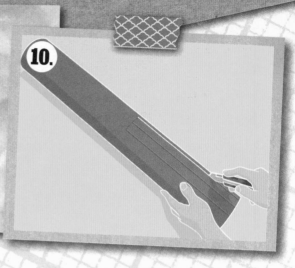

Step 11:

⚠ Place the tube over the outside corner of the tower so the cutout in the tube sits neatly on the edge. Hold and glue in place with the hot glue gun.

Step 12:

To make the roof for the top of the round tower, cut an arrow shape out of a scrap piece of cardboard, making the stem of the arrow the same width as the inside of the tube. Add some white craft glue to the sides and slip it into the top of the tube.

Step 13:

Draw a window at the front of the tower. Any shape or size will do, but make sure it's at the right height for your child to see out ⚠ of. Cut it out with a utility knife. Repeat steps 8 to 13 for the other tower, but this time gluing the packaging tube to the opposite side of the tower.

Step 14:

⚠ Arrange the three boxes so that the middle box with the drawbridge is set back a little and glue them together at the sides, using the hot glue gun. Glue the reserved pieces of square cardboard around the windows and drawbridge to create the look of stonework.

Step 15:

⚠ To make the pennant flag banner, cut a length of ribbon that is slightly longer than the distance between the tops of the round towers. Cut triangles from colored cardstock and staple to the top edges to the ribbon. Finally, staple the ends of the banner to the tops of the round towers.

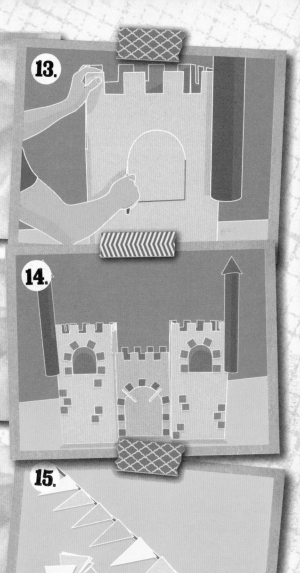

Step 16:

Add more round towers, flags, and windows and decorate as you want.

Pop-Pom Puppy

This pom-pom puppy has adorable droopy ears and a cute collar that can be adapted to any color ribbon or shape of bead that you want.

You will need:

- thick black yarn (body, about 1¼ ounces/35 g; head, about 1 ounce/25 g; binding for head and body, 32-inch/80-cm length)
- 4½-inch x 2¾-inch/12-cm x 7-cm piece of cardboard
- scissors
- yarn needle
- white craft glue
- templates from page 124
- black felt
- brown felt
- black embroidery thread
- 1 black plastic nose
- 2 black plastic eyes
- yellow ribbon
- 1 red star button

Time to make: about 30 minutes

Step 1:

Wrap the black yarn for the body around the cardboard.
Wrap it around with consistent and gentle tension,
making sure it is not too tight, and wrap it evenly
along the length of the cardboard. The wool shouldn't
be fatter in the middle. Tuck the end of the yarn into
the wrapped yarn. Gently slide the bundle of yarn off
the cardboard, making sure you hold it so that it
doesn't unravel. Using a 12-inch/30-cm length of yarn,
wrap it around the bundle horizontally, making sure it
is tight. It will squeeze the wrapped yarn together in
the middle.

⚠ Slide the blade of your scissors into the loops of the
bundle and gradually work your way around, until you
have a pom-pom.

Step 2:

⚠ Repeat Step 1 for the puppy's head, using less yarn to
create a slightly smaller pom-pom. Trim the smaller pom-
pom to form a neat round shape for the puppy's head. Trim
the larger pom-pom to create the puppy's body so that it
has a flat top and body and straighter sides.

Step 3:

⚠ Using a large needle threaded with an 8-inch/20-cm length
of yarn, thread the needle through the bottom of the body
and up through the head. Loop the yarn back through the
top of the head and through the body, then tie in a knot
at the bottom to hold them together. You can also dab glue
between the head and the body to make it extra secure
before sewing.

Photocopy or trace the templates on page 124. Using the
template as a guide, cut out the puppy's ears from the
black felt. Pinch the flat edge of the ears to form a pleat
and, using a needle and black thread, sew in place.

Step 4:

Add white craft glue to the pinched edge of the ears and wedge the ears into the side of the pom-pom head so that they droop downward.

Step 5:

Using the templates on page 124, cut out the puppy's nose from brown felt. Cut a little hole in the nose and insert the black bead nose. Add a black vertical stitch to the felt underneath the nose. Glue the black beads for the eyes and the nose to the puppy's head. Let dry.

Step 6:

Using the template on page 124 as a guide, cut out the puppy's feet from the black felt. Wedge the paws just above the bottom of the body pom-pom so that they can droop down a little instead of attaching them underneath the body. Finally, glue the red star button in place on the ribbon, wrap it around the puppy's neck, and glue at the back.

DAD TIP

This cute Pom-pom puppy is not suitable for children under three years of age, so give it only to older children.

Or you could...

Make the puppy's body from two different shades of yarn.
Draw a line halfway down the cardboard to act as a guide.
Wrap half the cardboard with white yarn and the other half
with black yarn. Trim the pom-pom so the white part is
smaller than the black, so he has a white belly.

Catapult Game

Become a pro at aiming with a catapult and target made from recycled materials.

Time to make:
1 hour

You will need:

- 2 aluminum foil or plastic wrap cardboard tubes (about 12 inches/30 cm long)
- ruler
- felt-tip pen
- cutting board
- ballpoint pen
- packaging tape
- small plastic dessert container
- 2 paper cups
- ½-inch/8-mm-diameter, 8-inch/20-cm-long wooden dowel (or similar, such as a chopstick)

- white craft glue, glue gun and glue sticks, or double-sided clear tape
- cereal box
- craft knife
- scissors
- 1 toilet roll tube, cut in half to make two small tubes
- 2 large wooden craft/ice pop sticks (about 6 inches/15 cm long)
- paint, pens, paintbrushes, to decorate as you want
- newspaper or magazine
- small plastic milk carton (optional)

Step 1:

Using a ruler, measure 4 inches/10 cm in from the left end of one of the cardboard tubes and make a mark with the felt-tip pen. Make another four marks at ¾-inch/2-cm intervals. Place the cardboard tube on a hard, flat surface, such as a cutting board, and hold securely with one hand. Using the ballpoint pen, carefully push and twist the pen nib into the first 4-inch/10-cm pen mark until you break through the tube. Rotate the pen so it makes a round hole. Repeat this on the remaining four pen marks.

Step 2:

Hold the end of the tube, making sure the holes are nowhere near your hand. Push the ballpoint pen into the first hole and gently twist and push so you start to make a hole in the opposite side of the tube. Push the pen right through the tube and rotate to make a round hole. Repeat this on the remaining holes, making sure your hand stays clear of the potential exit holes.

Step 3:

Tape the dessert container to the other end of the cardboard tube with packaging tape, making sure that the holes on the tube are centered on the sides of the container. First attach a piece of tape to each side of the container and the end of the tube, then wrap a longer piece of tape around tape at the end of the tube. Add a short piece to tape the bottom of the container to the tube, then wrap one more long piece around the ends of the tape on the tube. Set side.

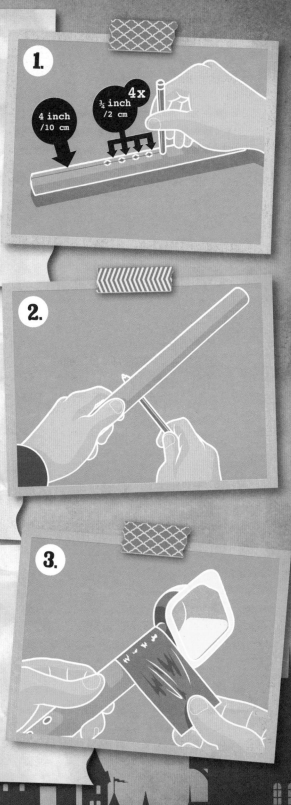

1.
4 inch /10 cm
¾ inch /2 cm
4x

2.

3.

Step 4:

⚠️ Take one of the paper cups and hold it upside down. Use the ballpoint pen to make a hole in the side about ½ inch/1 cm away from the bottom of the cup. Watch out for your hands. Continue to push the pen through the cup and out the opposite side. Twist the pen to make the hole round. Repeat on the other paper cup.

Step 5:

Push the dowel through one set of holes in the cardboard tube so that it sits with equal amounts protruding on each side. Now push the paper cups onto the ends of the dowel. The catapult is ready.

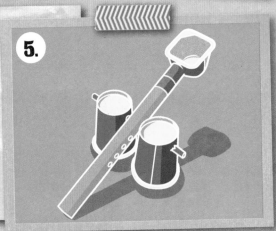

Step 6:

Either glue or use double-sided tape to seal the ends of the cereal box closed. Place it flat on a table so the back of the box is face down. Draw a line with a felt-tip pen and a ruler that is 1¼ inches/3 cm in from the left short edge, right short edge, and top long edge and a line 2 inches/5 cm up from the bottom long edge.

⚠ Use a craft knife to cut out the panel from the center of the box. Be careful and press gently when you do this, because the box could collapse. Keep the cardboard you cut out.

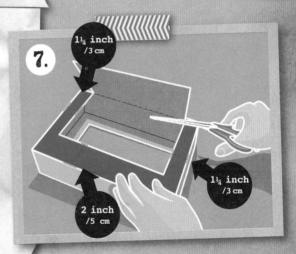

6.

1¼ inch /3 cm

1¼ inch /3 cm

2 inch /5 cm

Step 7:

Turn the box over. Using a felt-tip pen and ruler, draw a line 1¼ inches/3 cm in from the left short edge and right short edge and a line 2 inches/5 cm up from the bottom long edge. This time you don't need a line across the top.

⚠ Use a craft knife to cut out the panel from the center of the box, cutting along the top crease line of the box so that there isn't a border across the top. You may find it easier to cut the top edge with a pair of scissors.

7.

1¼ inch /3 cm

1¼ inch /3 cm

2 inch /5 cm

Step 8:

Place the box on one of its shorter ends, the larger border closest to you and the larger frame area to your right. On the top of the box, draw a line ¾ inch/2 cm in from the left long edge and a line ½ inch/1 cm up from the bottom short edge with a felt-tip pen and ruler. Place one end of the remaining cardboard tube in the middle of the two lines. Draw around the tube with a felt-tip pen to make a circle the size of the tube.

Step 9:

⚠ Using the craft knife, carefully cut out the hole. The box will be unstable at the ends, so don't press too heavily and keep your fingers away at all times. Reseal the edges with double-sided tape or glue, if necessary. Repeat the previous step on the opposite end of the box to create two holes that line up directly opposite each other.

Step 10:

Start to feed the cardboard tube into one end of the box through the hole you just made. As you do so, feed the two halves of the toilet roll onto it before pushing the cardboard tube through the opposite side of the box. You should have equal amounts of tube protruding from each side of the box.

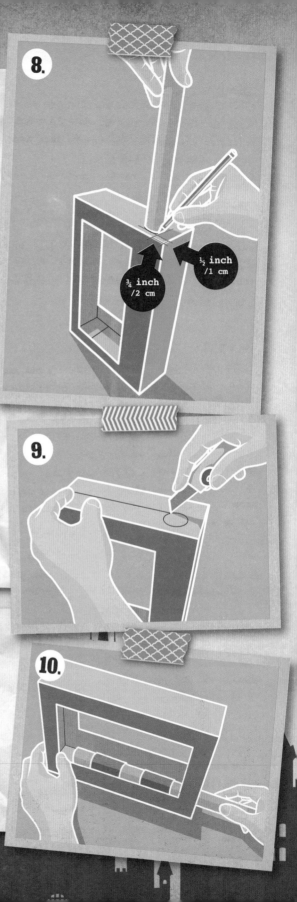

Step 11:

⚠️ Lay the box flat on the table with the side that has the frame on all four sides facing down. Glue a wooden craft/ice pop stick to one toilet roll half on the side closer to the frame at the bottom, making sure the top of the stick is covering the top frame. This is a little tricky, so take your time and check you have set it up correctly before applying the glue. Repeat with the other stick and toilet roll half.

Step 12:

When the box is upright, the wooden sticks should rest against the frame on the inside front of the box, as shown in the image.

Step 13:

Place one of the pieces of reserved cardboard, cut from the box earlier, plain side up on a table. Using a roll of package tape as a guide, draw two circles on the card with a felt-tip pen.

⚠️ Cut out the circle, using either scissors or the craft knife. If you are using a craft knife, be sure to protect the tabletop with a cutting board or scrap piece of cardboard.

Step 14:

Glue the disks to the front of the wooden sticks so they sit centered in the box window.

Now, it's time to decorate your catapult and target box with paint, pens, or whatever you choose.

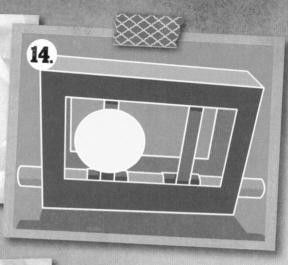

Step 15:

To make the projectiles, scrunch up a sheet of newspaper as tightly as you can. Try not to make the ball any bigger than the size of a golf ball.

DAD TIP

How to play:

Position your target box on the floor, a couple of yards away from you with the targets upright. Next, place your newspaper ball projectile into the plastic cup on the catapult. With one hand, hold one of the stands firmly. Take aim at the target and smack down on the end of the cardboard tube. Don't hit too hard or you'll squash the tube. Try to knock down the targets. Try adjusting the catapult to see how far your projectile will go. Just move the wooden dowel to a different hole position and try again. And remember, aim at a target and not a person.

Variation:

As an alternative to the target, you can make a "catcher" out of a plastic milk carton. ⚠️ Cut a cube shape from the bottom of the milk carton, leaving the handle and the bottom of the carton to look like a scoop. Just draw the cut lines with a permanent marker and then carefully cut the milk carton with a pair of scissors. One person catapults while the other person tries to catch the newspaper balls.

Crusher-Bot Puppet

Wreak havoc on the neighborhood with a Crusher-Bot puppet. You can make his jaws open and close and wiggle his arms.

You will need:

- small corrugated cardboard box (about 9 inches/23 cm wide x 6¼ inches/16 cm high x 4 inches/10 cm deep
- ruler
- pencil
- scissors or utility knife
- glue gun and glue sticks or double-sided clear tape
- ballpoint pen
- ball of string
- 6 table tennis balls
- piece of thick corrugated cardboard or small cutting board
- 3 toilet roll tubes (about 1½ inches/4 cm in diameter)
- template from page 126
- piece of thick corrugated cardboard, about 8 inches/20 cm square
- 4 wooden beads (about ¾ inch/2 cm)
- 1 tennis ball
- 1 large round coin
- 4 large wooden craft/ice pop sticks
- 4 buttons (about ¾ inch/2 cm)
- 4 lengths of strong thread (about 28 inches/70 cm long)
- paints and paintbrushes, stickers or tissue paper, to decorate as you want

Time to make: about **40 minutes**

Step 1:

Remove any tape, along with any stickers or labels, from the top and the bottom of the box. Open up the box, measure and mark with a pencil half the width on the short side of the box, and draw a line from the top to the bottom of the box on both sides. Cut along the line with a pair of scissors and repeat on the other side, so the box is in two halves.

Step 2:

Take one of the box halves and stick the flaps together with either a glue gun or double-sided tape to create an open top box. Repeat with the other box half.

Step 3:

On the front of each box, measure ¾ inch/ 2 cm down from the top open edge and draw a horizontal line with a pencil. For the teeth, draw an even number of vertical lines, equally spaced above the horizontal line. Mark out the squares to be cut out with a diagonal line. Using the scissors or utility knife, carefully cut out the alternate squares to look like teeth. Don't worry if they are uneven. Repeat on the other box.

Step 4:

Turn the boxes around so the teeth are facing away from you. Measure ½ inch/1.5 cm down from the top open edge and draw a line across the box width with a pencil. Measure 1¼ inches/ 3 cm in from both sides and make a mark. Use the ballpoint pen to make two small holes through the box. Repeat on the other box.

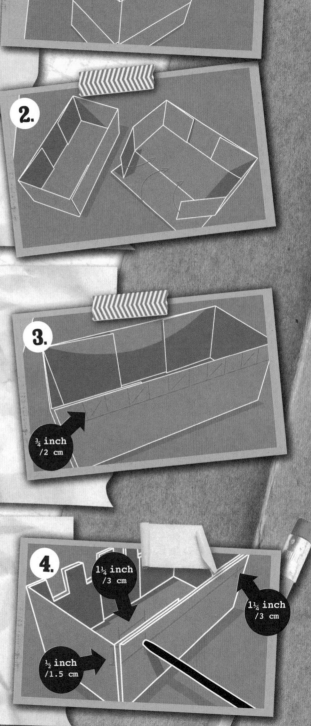

Step 5:

Place the two boxes on a table, back to back so the holes line up. Cut two pieces of string about 8 inches/20 cm long. Feed one end of one string through a pair of holes and tie the boxes together with a knot. Repeat with the other piece of string ⚠ and then trim the excess with scissors. Make sure the loops of string are loose so that the jaw opens and closes easily.

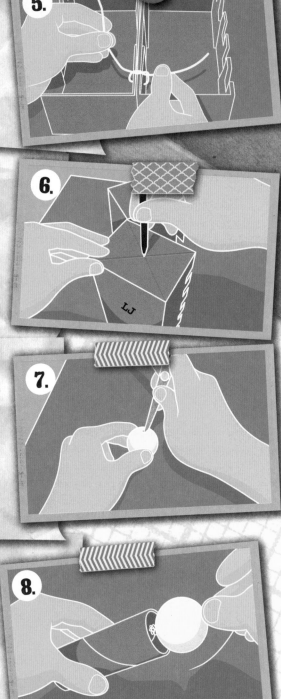

Step 6:

Decide which of the two boxes will be the lower jaw and write "LJ" in small letters on it. Using the ruler and pencil, draw a diagonal line on one of the shortest sides from one corner to the other of the lower jaw. Then draw a diagonal line from the opposite corners—where the lines cross will mark the center. Using a ballpoint pen, make a small hole where the lines cross. Do the same on the other short side of the lower jaw. This is where you will attach the arms. Set side.

Step 7:

⚠ Place one of the table tennis balls on a scrap piece of thick cardboard or a cutting board. With either the sharp point of a pair of scissors or a utility knife, make a small hole in the center that's big enough to thread string through. Be careful while doing this, making sure to press gently on the ball because it is thin. Make a hole on the opposite side of the ball to the first hole.

Step 8:

⚠ Cut a 12-inch/30-cm length of string and tie five or six knots at one end to make one large knot. Thread the other end of the string through the two holes in the table tennis ball.

Glue the table tennis ball to one end of a toilet roll tube, using the glue gun and making sure the knotted end of the string is inside the toilet roll. Use the glue gun to secure another table tennis ball to the other end of the toilet roll. Repeat steps 7 and 8 for the other arm.

Step 9:

Photocopy or trace the template on page 126 and using it as a guide, draw two shapes onto a piece of thick corrugated cardboard. Make sure the semicircle is the same size as the table tennis balls and that one is a mirror image of the other.

⚠️ Use the utility knife and a ruler to carefully cut out the grabbers. Use a glue gun to secure one of the grabbers to the end of one of the table tennis balls without the string. Glue it at a slight angle instead of straight. Repeat for the opposite arm.

Step 10:

Thread the string from one of the arms through the hole at the side of the lower jaw you made earlier. Thread one of the wooden beads onto the string and tie a knot to hold it in place. Make sure there is enough slack in the string so that the arm dangles down and there is plenty of movement. Repeat on the opposite side.

Step 11:

⚠️ Draw a line around the center of the tennis ball. Put the tennis ball onto a piece of thick corrugated cardboard or cutting board and use a utility knife to carefully cut it half, using the line as a guide. Take your time doing this because tennis balls are tough. Cut the remaining toilet roll tube in half, using either the scissors or utility knife, to create two equal-length tubes. Use the glue gun to secure one of the tubes to the top of half a ball. Repeat for the other half of the tube and ball.

Step 12:

Turn the Crusher-Bot head upside down so the lower jaw is uppermost.

⚠️ Glue the two feet onto the bottom of the jaw with the glue gun, making sure they are in the middle and spaced evenly. Once the glue has set, turn the Crusher-Bot the right way up. He should stand easily on his own two feet.

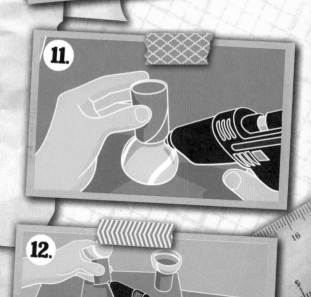

Step 13:

Measure the width of the head along the top front edge and make a pencil mark at the halfway point. Use a ballpoint pen to make a small hole where the pencil mark is at the top front edge.

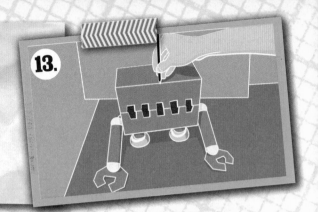

Step 14:

Draw a diagonal line from one corner to the opposite corner on the top of the head and then draw another diagonal line between the other two corners to find the center. Place a large coin in the center of the top of the head.

⚠ Draw around the coin and then use a utility knife to cut out a hole.

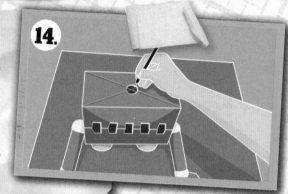

Step 15:

Turn Crusher-Bot upside down. Use a ruler to find the center and use a ballpoint pen to make a small hole in the center point. Turn Crusher-Bot the right way up.

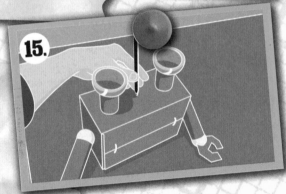

Step 16:

Take the last two table tennis balls and use the glue gun to attach them to the top front edge of Crusher-Bot, making sure they are about ½ inch/ 1 cm apart. Don't use too much glue, otherwise it will drip down the front of the head. Decorate and paint your Crusher-Bot however you want and set aside to dry.

Step 17:

⚠ Using the glue gun, add a line of glue along only half of the length of one of the wooden craft/ice pop sticks. Place another wooden stick on top and press firmly together. Let the glue dry completely.

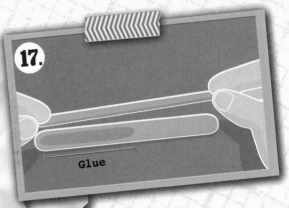

Glue

Step 18:

⚠ Gently pull apart the unglued ends of the wooden sticks. Carefully push a wooden bead into the open end, making sure the hole is visible between the sticks, and then use the glue gun to secure it in place. Hold the bead while the glue sets, making sure you don't get any on your fingers. Add some more glue to make sure the bead is secured well in place. Set aside to dry completely.

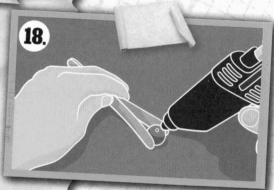

Step 19:

⚠ Glue the ends of the other two wooden sticks together, overlapping by about 1¾ inches/4 cm. Let the glue set before proceeding. Then cut a small "V" shape about ½ inch/1 cm from the ends of the wooden sticks, using a really sharp pair of pointed scissors. Set the sticks aside.

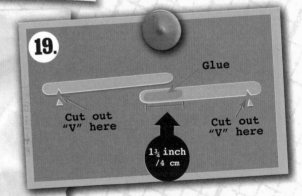

Glue

Cut out "V" here

Cut out "V" here

1¾ inch /4 cm

Step 20:

⚠ Glue the two wooden stick parts together to form a cross, as shown in the diagram. Make sure the two halves are glued really well together. The hole in the bead should be facing upward.

Step 21:

⚠️ Cut four 28-inch/70-cm lengths of strong thread. Securely tie a button at the end of each one. Trim any excess thread from the ends.

Step 22:

Open up the head of Crusher-Bot. Feed one length of thread and button up through the hole in the middle of the lower jaw, so the button is on the outside. Then continue to feed the string through the large hole in the top of the head. Close the head and pull the string until it stops. Tie the string you've just pulled up through the head and to the center of the wooden stick cross. Tie it ⚠️ tightly, making sure you have only a small amount of excess thread, before trimming it with scissors.

Step 23:

Open up the head again and push a second thread through the small hole between Crusher-Bot's eyes. Pull it through until it's stopped by the button. Feed it through the bead on the end of the wooden stick cross. Tie the last wooden bead to the thread, making sure that when you hold the wooden stick cross directly above Crusher-Bot's head, the bead is hovering about ½ inch/1 cm above the bead that is glued to the cross.

Step 24:

Using the ballpoint pen, make a small hole in the outer claw of each grabber. Feed one of the lengths of thread and button through the hole you just made and then tie the other end to the end of the arm of the wooden stick cross, where you cut the "V" shape earlier. Repeat on the other arm. When you hold the wooden stick cross above his head, the arms should hang outstretched. If they are a little low, just wind the thread around the wooden stick a couple of times and you're done. You can open his jaw by pulling the bead.

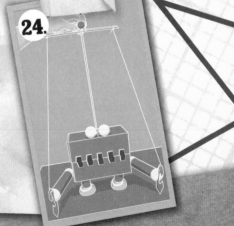

DAD TIP

Decorate Crusher-Bot with poster paint and stickers or glue tissue paper onto him. Add a black dot to the center of his eyes with a black felt-tip pen or you could even make a girl Crusher-Bot by painting lashes around the eyes.

Imaginative Questions

Create some interesting questions that you can put in a jar to spark up new conversations with your child.

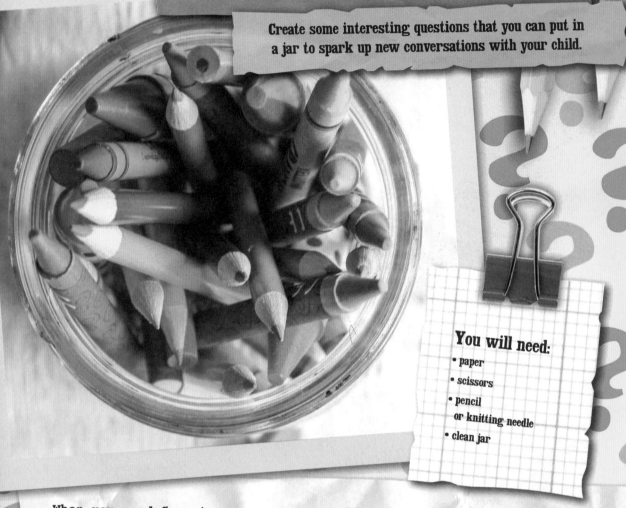

You will need:
- paper
- scissors
- pencil
  or knitting needle
- clean jar

When you need five minutes' peace, chances are that your child will be as noisy as a tornado. However, when you do want a conversation and to find out more about their day—for example, on their return from school or a sleepover—more often than not they become mute. Questions, such as "What did you do today?," are always met with "Not sure. I can't remember."

There is, however, a wonderful game you can play to spark up new, fun conversations with your child. It involves creating some interesting questions that you put in a jar and pick out at random. We've listed some suggestions here to get you started, but you can make up your own to put into the jar. You can be either surreal and amusing or choose questions that will get an honest and emotional response.

DAD TIP

To keep interest up, you could put a couple of prize slips in the jar. Instead of a question, notes could say "YOU WIN...".

GETTING STARTED

First, put all your questions down on paper. Either handwrite them or type them and print them out. Once you've done that, cut your questions into little slips. Wrap the slips around a pencil or knitting needle to create a swirl that can be uncurled when you pull the questions out. Put your springy swirls into the jar and it's that easy.

WARNING: You may never be able to shut up your child again!

QUESTION IDEAS:

- If you could have a pet alligator, where would you keep him?
- What was the best dream you have ever had?
- If you could be any type of ice cream, what would you be?
- What is the last thing that made you smile?
- How would you describe yourself to someone who hasn't met you?
- What's the biggest dog you've ever seen?
- If you could have a power like a superhero, what power would you like?
- What is the yuckiest thing you've ever eaten?
- What is your greatest dance move?

- If you were a dinosaur, what would you smell like?
- When was the last time you were really muddy?
- If you could change your name, what would you like to be called?
- What is the first thing you can ever remember?
- What is the biggest surprise you've ever had?
- If you were a witch, who would you turn into a toad?
- Where is your favorite place in the world?
- When was the last time you got really silly?
- What is your favorite thing that Mom does with you?
- If you could drive a car, where would you drive to?
- What color is the happiest color?
- If you could be any flavor of potato chips, what would you be?
- Would you rather travel back in time or through space?
- What's the funniest face you can pull?
- What is your favorite movie?
- If you were invisible for a day, what would you do?
- What sound annoys you the most?
- If you could go to the moon, what is the first thing you would do there?
- Would you rather be too hot or too cold?
- Why don't monkeys live in houses?
- Who is the funniest person you know?
- If you were the richest person in the world, what would you do with all your money?
- What's the worst smell you've ever smelled?
- Would you rather be able to fly or be invisible?

- If you could make three wishes, what would they be?
- What is the coolest thing you have ever seen?
- How many hugs do you need every day?
- If you were to put any question in this jar, what would you go for?
- What is your favorite day in the week?
- If you could be any animal, which one would you be?
- What do you want to be when you grow up?
- If you could keep only one toy, which one would you keep?

DAD TIP

You could include some challenges or dares in the jar as well. So, you could write on the slip "Now, do a jumping jack!" or "Name five things beginning with D."

Get Creative in the Kitchen

Become a chef for the day with these fun recipes.

Children can have loads of fun creating in the kitchen—especially if they get to taste the results afterward. Although half of the effort can involve stopping your child from eating all of the ingredients before they are baked, cooking with your child is a rewarding and entertaining experience. It can also be as creative as you want if there is decoration involved—your child will love adding edible sparkles and frostings to baked cookies and cakes, and you can encourage them to choose their favorite colors and shapes for decorating. Safety is important in the kitchen, too, so make sure your child stays well away from the oven when it is hot and supervise them closely at all times. Your child will develop an understanding of how food is produced, as well as getting a great treat after all the hard work is done. Start baking!

You will need:

- 1 cup all-purpose flour, sifted
- 1¼ teaspoons baking powder
- 1 stick unsalted butter, cut into small pieces, softened
- ½ cup granulated sugar
- 2 extra-large eggs, lightly beaten
- pink, white, and red sprinkles, to decorate
- 10 pink drinking straws, cut to 3½ inches/9 cm long, to serve

Buttercream

- 1 stick unsalted butter, softened
- 1¾ cup confectioners' sugar
- 1 tablespoon lemon juice
- a few drops of pink liquid food coloring

- 10-hole cupcake pan
- 10 paper cupcake liners
- sifter
- large bowl
- electric handheld mixer
- tablespoon
- oven mitts
- wire rack
- medium bowl
- spatula
- plate

FIZZY PINK CUPCAKES

Step 1:

Preheat the oven to 350°F/180°C. Line a cupcake pan with ten paper cupcake liners. Put the flour and baking powder into a large bowl. Add the butter, granulated sugar, and eggs and beat together, using an electric mixer, until the mixture is pale and fluffy.

Step 2:

Using a tablespoon, spoon the batter into the liners. Bake in the preheated oven for 15—20 minutes, until risen and golden. Remove from the oven and let cool a little. Transfer to a wire rack.

Step 3:

For the buttercream, beat together the butter, confectioners' sugar, and lemon juice in a medium bowl with an electric mixer. Stir in a few drops of pink food coloring to create a pale-pink color.

Step 4:

Thickly swirl the frosting over the tops of the cupcakes, using a spatula. Put the sprinkles on a plate, hold onto the paper liners, and roll the cupcake edges in the sprinkles. Push a straw into the top of the cupcakes to decorate.

Makes: 12

You will need:

- 1 stick butter, softened, plus extra for greasing
- ½ cup granulated sugar
- ½ cup packed light brown sugar
- 1 extra-large egg
- 1 teaspoon vanilla extract
- 1¼ cups all-purpose flour
- ¼ cup unsweetened cocoa powder
- ½ teaspoon baking powder

Chocolate sauce

- 1 cup heavy cream
- 2 tablespoons milk
- 4 ounces semisweet chocolate, chopped

To serve

- 1 (1-pint) container vanilla ice cream
- gold and silver star sprinkles
- 12 mini candles

- 12-cup muffin pan
- large bowl
- electric handheld mixer
- sifter
- wooden spoon
- teaspoon
- oven mitts
- spatula
- wire rack
- small saucepan

Step 1:

⚠ Preheat the oven to 350°F/180°C. Grease a 12-cup cupcake pan. Put the butter, sugars, egg, and vanilla into a large bowl and use an electric mixer to beat together until the mixture is light and fluffy. Sift the flour, cocoa, and baking powder over the top and stir together with a wooden spoon to make a firm batter.

Step 2:

Use a wet teaspoon to divide the batter into 12 portions and place into the muffin pan cups. Press the batter up the sides of each of the muffin cups—it should look a little coarse around the edges.

Step 3:

⚠ Bake in the preheated oven for 15–18 minutes or until the cakes are just firm at the edges. Let cool in the pan for 5 minutes. Carefully run a spatula around the edge of each cake to loosen it from the pan. Transfer to a wire rack to cool completely.

Step 4:

⚠ To make the "lava" chocolate sauce, heat the cream and milk together in a small saucepan until almost boiling. Remove from the heat, add the chocolate, and stir until a smooth sauce forms. Set aside but keep warm.

Step 5:

⚠ To serve, place a warm cake "volcano" on a plate, top with a scoop of vanilla ice cream, and make a "lava flow" with the chocolate sauce. Sprinkle with gold and silver star sprinkles. Finally, place a candle in the center of each cake and light carefully. Bring to the table with the candle lit for best effect.

DAD TIP

Sparklers or fountain candles would also look great. Choose ones that are especially designed for cakes and keep children at a distance.

SWEETHEART COOKIES

Makes: 32

You will need:

- 1¾ sticks unsalted butter, softened
- ¾ cup granulated sugar
- 1 extra-large egg
- 2 teaspoons vanilla extract
- 3¼ cups all-purpose flour

Royal icing

- 3⅔ cups confectioners' sugar
- 2 tablespoons plus 1 teaspoon egg white powder
- ⅓ cup cold water
- 4 food coloring gels, such as bright red, pink, blue, and mauve

- 2 large bowls
- electric handheld mixer
- wooden spoon
- sifter
- plastic wrap
- parchment paper
- 3 baking sheets
- rolling pin
- selection of heart-shape cutters
- spatula
- oven mitts
- wire rack
- 5 small bowls
- toothpicks
- pastry bag and No. 3 or 4 tip
- 4 squeeze bottles

Step 1:

⚠ Put the butter and sugar into a large bowl and mix well with an electric mixer. Beat in the egg and vanilla extract with a wooden spoon. Sift in the flour and mix everything together to make a coarse dough. Form the dough into a ball with your hands, wrap it in plastic wrap, and chill in the refrigerator for at least 10 minutes.

Step 2:

⚠ Line three baking sheets with parchment paper. Unwrap the dough and place between two sheets of parchment paper. Roll out to an even thickness of ¼ inch/5 mm, turning the dough occasionally. Press out different-size cookies using the heart cutters, gathering up the scraps and rerolling the dough as necessary.

Step 3:

⚠ Using a spatula, transfer the cookies onto the lined baking sheets. Chill in the refrigerator for 10 minutes—this will help to prevent them from spreading during baking. Meanwhile, preheat the oven to 350°F/180°C.

Step 4:

⚠ Bake the cookies in the preheated oven for 15–18 minutes, until just turning golden at the edges. Cool on the baking sheets for a few minutes before transferring to a wire rack to cool completely. Lower the oven temperature to 250°F/120°C to be ready for Step 8.

Step 5:

⚠ To make the royal icing, sift the confectioners' sugar into a large bowl and add the egg white powder and water. Stir with a wooden spoon until thickening and the confectioners' sugar has dissolved. Now use an electric mixer to beat the icing for 3–4 minutes, until it is thick, like toothpaste.

Step 6:

Divide the icing in two and put into two small bowls. Color one half red by gradually adding food coloring gel with the tip of a toothpick and kneading to an even color, and keep the other white. Spoon one-third of the red icing into a pastry bag fitted with a No. 3 or 4 plain tip. Carefully pipe a red icing border around the edge of each cookie and let set for 10 minutes.

Step 7:

To make a "flood" icing, add water to the white and red icings, a drop at a time and beating between additions, until the icing is the consistency of thick yogurt. Divide the white icing into three and color each third a different color. Spoon the icings into squeeze bottles fitted with plain tips.

Step 8:

⚠ Working on a few cookies at a time, direct the icings inside the piped borders. Then pipe a few spots or lines in the other icing colors and use a toothpick to feather the contrasting icing. Gently tap the cookies to make any air bubbles rise to the surface and pop these with a toothpick. Repeat with the rest of the cookies and icings. Return the cookies to the low oven and dry out for about 40 minutes or until the icing is set.

DINOSAUR SKELETON COOKIES

You will need:

- 1¾ sticks unsalted butter, softened
- ¾ cup packed light brown sugar
- 1 extra-large egg
- 2 tablespoons black molasses
- 3¼ cups all-purpose flour
- ½ teaspoon ground ginger
- ½ teaspoon ground cinnamon

Royal icing

- 1¼ cups confectioners' sugar
- 2 teaspoons egg white powder
- 2 tablespoons cold water

- parchment paper
- 2 baking sheets
- large bowl
- electric handheld mixer
- sifter
- wooden spoon
- plastic wrap
- rolling pin
- assorted dinosaur cutters
- spatula
- oven mitts
- wire rack
- medium bowl
- pastry bag and No. 2 or 3 tip

Step 1:

⚠ Line two baking sheets with parchment paper. In a large bowl, cream the butter and sugar with an electric mixer until just coming together. Add the egg and molasses and briefly beat together. Sift in the flour, ground ginger, and ground cinnamon, and mix with a wooden spoon to make a coarse dough. Gather it into a ball with your hands, wrap in plastic wrap, and chill in the refrigerator for at least 10 minutes.

Step 2:

⚠ Roll out the dough between two large sheets of parchment paper to an even thickness of ¼ inch/5 mm, turning the dough occasionally. Press out 28 dinosaur shapes using the cutters, rerolling the dough as necessary. Using a spatula, transfer the cookies to the lined baking sheets, leaving a little space between each. Chill in the refrigerator for 10 minutes. Meanwhile, preheat the oven to 350°F/180°C.

Step 3:

⚠ Bake in the preheated oven for 15—18 minutes, until just turning golden at the edges. Let cool on the baking sheets for a few minutes before transferring to a wire rack to cool completely. Reduce the oven temperature to 250°F/120°C to be ready for Step 5.

DAD TIP

To pipe the skeleton shapes, start with the main bones on each dinosaur, then add the smaller bones for extra detail.

Step 4:

⚠️ To make the royal icing, sift the confectioners' sugar and egg white powder into a medium bowl, add the water, then use a wooden spoon to gently stir the mixture until all the powder has dissolved. Now use an electric mixer to beat the mixture for 3–4 minutes, until the icing is thick, like toothpaste. Spoon the icing into a pastry bag fitted with a No. 2 or 3 piping tip and pipe skeleton shapes onto the cookies.

Step 5:

⚠️ Place the cookies on baking sheets and dry out in the low oven for about 40 minutes, or until nice and hard. Remove from the oven and let cool for a few minutes before transferring to a wire rack to cool completely.

Shadow Puppet Theater

Create your own little characters and put on a show
with this really easy-to-make puppet theater.

You will need:

- 3 similar-size cereal boxes
- double-sided clear tape
- ruler
- pen or pencil
- craft knife or scissors
- 11 x 14-inch/28 x 35 cm sheet
  of tracing paper
- template on page 127
- wooden craft/ice pop sticks
- flashlight or table lamp
- paints, paintbrushes, and
  pens, to decorate as you want

Time to make:
about 30 minutes

Step 1:

Seal up the open end of one of the cereal boxes, using double-sided tape. Lay the box flat and draw lines ¾ inch/2 cm in from each edge of the top face of the box with a ruler and pen or pencil. Carefully ⚠ cut out the rectangle using a craft knife or scissors.

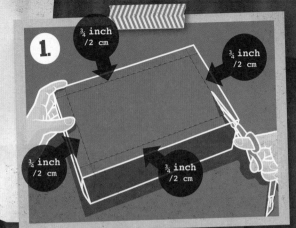

Step 2:

Turn the box over and draw lines ¾ inch/2 cm in from one of the long sides and two of the short sides. ⚠ Cut along the lines you've just drawn down to the bottom edge of the box and cut along the bottom edge.

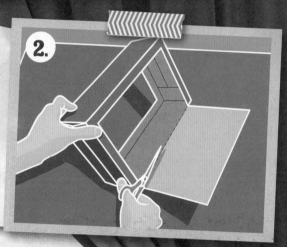

Step 3:

Place ¾-inch/2-cm lengths of double-sided tape on the four corners of the side of the box with the borders on all four sides. Carefully lay a sheet of tracing paper as flat as possible on top of the box and rub the corners to secure the paper to the tape, making sure the paper doesn't buckle or crease.

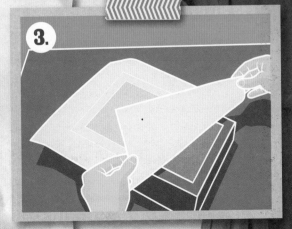

Step 4:

⚠ Trim the sides of the paper to the size of the box.

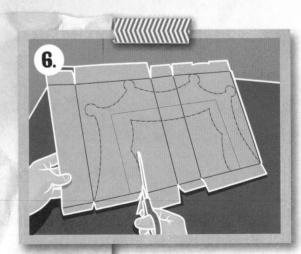

Step 5:

Open up the second cereal box and lay it out flat on a table with the printed side facing down. Place your theater box onto the cardboard and draw around the outside with either a pen or pencil. Remove the theater box and set aside.

Step 6:

Draw the outline of a theater front that is bigger than the rectangle you've just drawn. The curtains on the sides should slightly overlap the border of the theater box. Cut out the theater ⚠ front, using scissors.

Step 7:

Place the theater box on a table with the tracing paper facing down and put double-sided tape down the borders of the short sides. Leave the top edge without any tape.

Step 8:

Carefully place the theater front on top of the box and tape, keeping it centered and lining up the bottom of the theater front with the bottom of the theater box.

Step 9:

Open the last cereal box out flat. Measure the height and width of the theater box. Add 1½ inches/4 cm to the height, take away 1½ inches/4 cm from the width, and draw out a rectangular shape with those dimensions onto the flat box. For example, if the theater box is 8 inches/20 cm high x 12 inches/30 cm wide, draw a rectangle 9½ inches/24 cm high x 10½ inches/26 cm wide. Cut the rectangle out and slide it into the slot between the theater box and front.

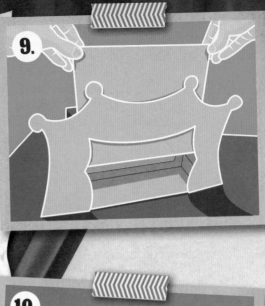

Step 10:

Photocopy or trace the puppet templates on page 127, or draw your own puppet shapes, if you prefer, on a scrap piece of cardboard. Cut out the puppets with scissors, then attach them at the back to wooden craft/ice pop sticks, using double-sided tape. Decorate the front of the theater however you want.

Step 11:
Place your theater on the edge of a table, in front of a table lamp or flashlight set up to shine a light behind the theater. Hold up your puppets behind the tracing paper to cast a shadow and create a shadow puppet show.

11.

DAD TIP

For more ideas on how to be creative with your shadow puppet theater, see pages 14–15.

Monster Truck

You can't beat a car that you can wear! This mini Monster Truck is made to measure with ribbons that slip over the shoulders.

You will need:

- glue gun and glue sticks
- large, rectangular, corrugated cardboard box
- ruler
- pencil
- utility knife
- ballpoint pen
- craft knife or scissors
- medium, rectangular, corrugated cardboard box
- template for the windscreen on page 125
- large cereal box, same width as the medium box
- cardboard egg carton
- scrap cardstock sheets
- large dinner plate (about 12 inches/30 cm in diameter)
- 9 paper plates (about 9 inches/23 cm in diameter)
- 4 paper towel cardboard tubes
- stapler
- orange or red tissue paper
- aluminum foil
- clear tape
- 5 toilet roll tubes
- 4 small foil pie dishes
- 2 lengths of wide ribbon (24 inches/60 cm long)
- paints and paintbrushes, crayons, and felt-tip pens, to decorate as you want

Time to make: about 40 minutes

DAD TIP

The suggested size of the large box is around 20 inches/51 cm long x 12½ inches/31 cm wide x 12½ inches/31 cm high with the flaps closed. However, the size of box you use depends on the size of your child and could be smaller or larger than this. It needs to be rectangular and landscape in shape and big enough to fit over your child with the top edge of the top flaps coming to around waist height.

Step 1:

⚠️ Glue down the flaps on the bottom of the large, rectangular box with a glue gun. Make sure to only apply a line of glue along the short edges of the long flaps, as shown by the blue lines.

Step 2:

Measure with a ruler about 3¼ inches/8 cm in from the short edges of the box and draw a line with a pencil.

⚠️ Use a utility knife and ruler to cut along these two lines, making sure you cut through the underlying flaps, too.

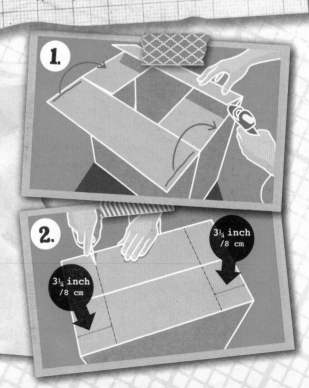

1.

2. 3¼ inch /8 cm   3¼ inch /8 cm

Step 3:

⚠️ Fold the flaps down inside the box and glue them to the sides with a glue gun. This will reinforce the sides a little. Turn the box over.

Step 4:

To make the hood of the Monster Truck, draw a diagonal line across one of the long flaps at about a 45-degree angle with a ballpoint pen and ruler. Push hard with the pen to score the surface of the cardboard, making it easier to fold the cardboard. Repeat on the opposite flap.

Step 5:

Lift the flaps up and bend them over.

⚠️ Use the glue gun to secure the short flap on top of the two bent flaps to create the slope of the hood. Trim off any excess cardboard above the hood you've just created from the two long flaps. Draw a line with a pencil and ruler to use as a guide and trim, using a utility knife.

Step 6:

To make the windshield, open up the smaller cardboard box and lay it out flat. Adjust the size of the template for the windshield (see page 125) on a photocopier so that the width matches the width of the hood of your box.

⚠️ Using the template as a guide, draw around it onto the cardboard and cut it out. Glue the long tab to the inside, top edge of the hood and the two side tabs to the inside of the box, so that there is a slight slope to the front of the windshield.

Step 7:

⚠️ Cut a couple of squares, measuring about 3¼ inches/ 8 cm x 3¼ inches/8 cm, from some scrap cardboard and fold them in half. Glue one of them to the inside corner of the side and back flap to hold them together. Repeat on the opposite side.

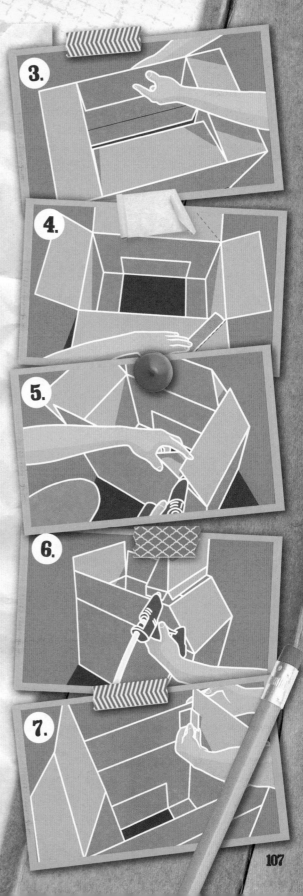

Step 8:

⚠️ To make the wings, glue together only the top flaps of the open end of the cereal box. Draw a diagonal line across both ends of the cereal box with a pencil and ruler, making sure they are exactly opposite. Cut the box with a craft knife or scissors along one of the diagonal lines and down the length of the box along the crease. Continue to cut along the other diagonal line and finally along the opposite crease of the length of the box. You should now have two identical halves of a box.

Step 9:

⚠️ After cutting the box, the end flaps will no longer be held together. Glue the side flaps of one of the box halves so that the angles of the corners of the short sides are slightly greater than 90 degrees. This will hold the wings at a slight angle.

Step 10:

⚠️ Glue this part to the back of the truck to stand as high as possible above the box. Glue the flaps of the other half of the box together and glue it to sit on top of the wings stand that you've just created.

Step 11:

⚠️ Cut the lid off the egg carton and cut off the highest points from the inside of the lid to make it level. Trim around the edges with scissors to tidy it up, so that you are just left with the six egg cups.

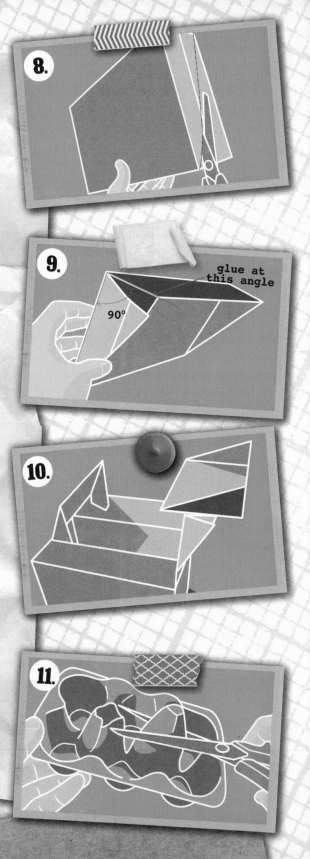

Step 12:

⚠ Glue the egg carton to the hood of the truck to look like an engine intake.

Step 13:

⚠ To make the wheels, use a dinner plate as a guide to draw a circle about 12 inches/30 cm in diameter, or larger than the paper plates, on some scrap cardboard. Cut out the circle with scissors. Glue a paper plate to one side and another to the opposite side of the cardboard circle, making sure they are centered. Repeat another three times. Lay the box on its side and glue two of the wheels to the lower half of the truck, so that they protrude evenly over the front, back, and bottom edges of the box. Let the glue set and then repeat on the other side, so that the wheels are level.

Step 14:

⚠ To make the exhaust pipes, flatten one end of one of the paper towel cardboard tubes. Use a stapler to staple the end closed. Repeat with the other three tubes.

Step 15:

⚠ Glue two exhaust pipes to each side of the truck. Add flames by scrunching up the orange tissue paper, adding glue to the end and pushing it down the ends of the tubes.

Step 16:

To make a shiny bumper, measure out a piece of scrap cardstock that is 2 inches/5 cm longer than the width of the truck and about 4 inches/ 10 cm wide and then add another 2 inches/5 cm to both ends.

⚠ Cut it out with scissors and crease the cardstock at the 2-inch/5-cm marks. Wrap the cardstock with aluminum foil, securing it with tape.

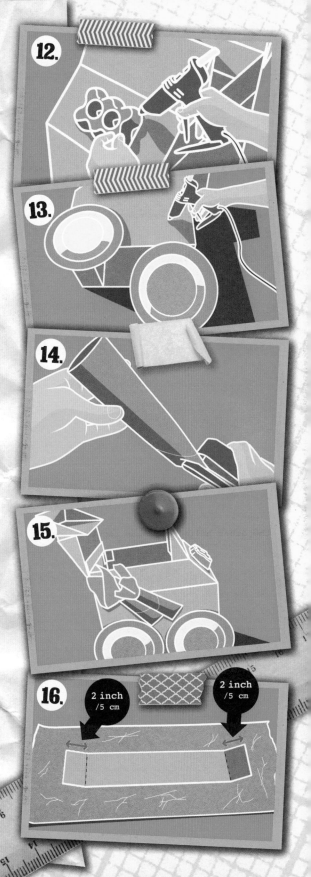

2 inch /5 cm

2 inch /5 cm

Step 17:

Draw around two toilet roll tubes onto the back of the bumper. Using the circles you've just drawn as a guide, cut two holes a little bigger than the diameter of the toilet roll tubes in only the foil, making sure you don't cut through the cardstock. Glue the two toilet tubes to the bumper in the holes you've just cut in the foil. You may need to cut the length of the tubes down a little if the bumper sits too far off the front of the truck. Repeat steps 16 and 17 for the rear bumper, then glue the bumpers to the front and back of the truck.

Step 18:

To make the steering wheel, glue a toilet roll tube to the back of a paper plate. Glue the open end of the toilet roll to the inside of the truck at the front.

Step 19:

Glue two small foil pie dishes to the front of the truck to create lights. Repeat with two more foil pie dishes at the back.

Step 20:

Glue one end of one of the ribbons to the back of a 2-inch/5-cm x 2-inch/5-cm square of scrap corrugated cardboard. Then glue the cardboard to the inside edge of the truck at only the front. Get your child to stand in the truck and hold it so that the wheels are just off the ground. Glue the other end of the ribbon to the inside of the box at the back to create a loop over your child's shoulders. Do the same with the other ribbon. Your child should be able to walk without the wheels scraping on the floor. Decorate the truck as you want and then it's ready to wear.

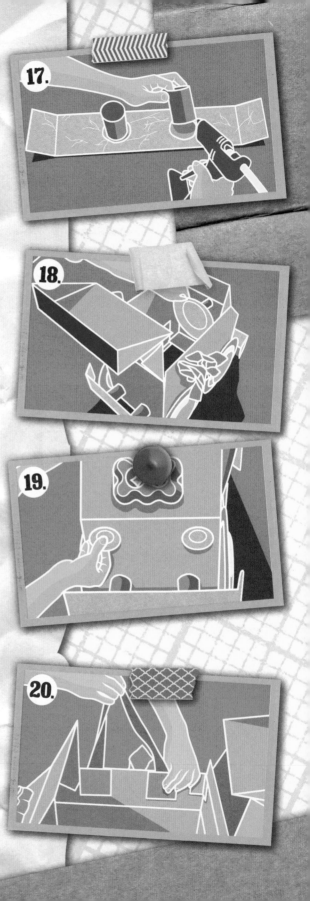

DAD TIP

There are plenty of areas to glue in this project, which must be done by an adult with a glue gun to hold them securely. Your child can help with the drawing and measuring, and they will love decorating the Monster Truck at the end.

Cora the Sock Caterpillar

Make a fun caterpillar out of a sock!

You will need:

- 1 colorful striped sock
- toy polyester filling
- thread (or yarn) and needle
- scissors
- buttons (or felt and glue)

 Time to make: about 30 minutes

CREATING THE FIRST SEGMENT

Push a small amount of toy polyester filling down into the toe of the sock. Keep adding more, a little at a time, until the foot of the sock is halfway full. Wrap a piece of thread or yarn around the sock, just behind the stuffing. Pull it tight and tie in a firm knot. You should now have a ball shape in the bottom of the sock.

CREATING THE SECOND SEGMENT

Add more toy polyester filling to the foot of the sock, stopping just before you get to the heel. Tie thread or yarn around the sock to hold the stuffing in place, as before.

CREATING THE THIRD SEGMENT AND THE HEAD

Stuff the heel of the sock and tie in place with thread or yarn, as before, to make a third ball shape. Repeat to make one last segment. This will be the head. You should now have four segments in total, plus an extra piece of sock at the top.

MAKING THE ANTENNAE

⚠ Divide the extra piece of sock in half by making two cuts down toward the head. Stop just before you reach the tied thread or yarn. This leaves you with two flaps.

⚠ Cut one of the flaps into three equal pieces, then stretch each one to make them all slightly longer. Braid the three pieces together (see below), then tie thread or yarn into a bow around the end to secure. (You might need someone to hold the caterpillar for you while you braid.) Repeat with the other flap to create a second antenna.

HOW TO BRAID

Move the right-hand strip to the left, taking it over the middle strip and pulling it tight. Then, move the left-hand strip to the right, taking it over the middle strip and pulling tight. Repeat, moving the right-hand strip over the middle one again. Keep going, taking it in turns to move the right and left-hand strips over the one in the middle, until you run out of material.

ADDING THE FINISHING TOUCHES

⚠ To make the eyes, sew on some buttons or glue two felt circles into place.

DAD TIP

This sock toy is not suitable for children under three years of age.

I Am Great!

When children draw themselves, they will often create something unusual. Fifteen arms, ears for eyes, monkey tails, and faces breathing fire—it can be nothing short of bizarre and hilarious. These creations aren't just down to a simple lack of pen control—a large part of it is because most children don't have a clear sense of self and aren't limited by self-consciousness. With that in mind, creating a stunning self-portrait with your child can be an incredibly rewarding activity for both you and them. You will start to explore how your child views themselves and create something that will hopefully last a long time, as well as have a lot of laughter along the way. And remember, this isn't just going to be a self-portrait; this is an "I Am Great" portrait.

You will need:

- sheet of paper or cardstock
- photo of your child (optional)
- paint
- paintbrushes
- pens, crayons, or coloring pencils
- glue
- magazines or photos

For the time capsule:

- plastic container, plastic bag, tape, relevant items, such as a newspaper (see list on page 119).

DRAW YOUR PICTURE

Using whatever medium your child feels happiest with (paint, pens, crayons, or coloring pencils), ask your child to draw a picture of themselves in the center of a large piece of paper or cardstock. The bigger the better, but 8½ x 11 inches/ 22 x 28 cm or larger will be fine. If your child has a photo of themselves that they particularly like, they could use it instead—just print out the photo and attach it in the center of the paper. Once you've done this first step, you can start to get really creative as you decorate the portrait.

ADD YOUR WORDS

Take out a second piece of paper or cardstock. Ask your child to write a brief description of who they are or some phrases that sum them up. This can be anything from between two or three lines to a few paragraphs, depending on your child's age and their love of creative writing. For younger children, you can write down the description for them as you lead them through a discussion where they talk about themselves. From the self-description, select five to ten words together that capture their feelings about themselves. Paint or write those around the portrait or photo on the other piece of cardstock.

DAD TIP

For a really up-to-date photo, perhaps you could get your child to take a selfie with your phone or tablet and print it out. You could also take a photo of your child holding up today's newspaper if you are planning to use the portrait in a time capsule.

DAD TIP

Portraits like these are a great activity to do on a rainy day, because they can be created completely inside the home.

GET BUSY WITH THE DECORATION

Gather together some decorative items that you can glue down around the portrait to illustrate it. This can include pictures, such as magazine images, photos, and drawings, as well as decorative items that you find around your house, such as candy wrappers, stickers, or ribbons. Get together anything that will help make the portrait a real reflection of the child and their interests. You can have a lot of fun with this—the goal is for the portrait to be a reflection of all of the different aspects of your child's life. So, if they like music, add musical notes, or if they like football, add photos of their favorite team. You can also be slightly more abstract with this project. For example, if you have decided your child is brave, you might want to add a picture of a lion, or if your child is funny, add some pictures of people laughing.